MW00958919

Teach and Learn with Technology

Theory and Application of Classroom

Technology Integration

Jill Outka-Hill, M.Ed.

Dedication

To the countless number of students I have taught, coached, mentored, and facilitated over my lifetime. It was an honor to have an impact on each and every one of you. You all taught me as much as I taught you

Preface

Technology has changed the way classrooms operate. Twenty years ago only a select few had access to technology and now every student and every teacher has an abundance of technology at their fingertips. Educators are not only expected to model technology use on a daily basis but also teach future generations how to use it safely, effectively, and efficiently.

Everyone in the education field knows "lifelong learning" is how we operate and as the world changes we adapt, we learn, and we teach. That is why it is so important for educators to learn how to implement technology into their classrooms even if we don't know everything there is to know about it. Chances are, if we get stuck, a student will help us out.

The students walking the hallways and playing on the playgrounds in schools today are the great leaders of tomorrow. These students will be faced with problems we can't fathom today. These students will have careers that don't exist today, and be required to do jobs that we don't understand today.

As educators, how do we prepare these students for such an unknown future?

This book is about the theory and application of technology integration into education. Although I will mention specific technology tools throughout the book, it is NOT about learning new tools. Tech tools will come and they will go. I have seen the evolution over the past 20 years of teaching students from age 4 to 94. I have seen technology fill our schools, homes, and workplaces and I have seen successful technology integration make all the difference to both teachers and their students. This pedagogical practice begins with the willingness to try new things, fail, and learn from those failures together with your students.

I began teaching adult software classes over 20 years ago. For the past 16 years I have been a technology facilitator at an elementary school and an adjunct instructor at a local community college where I taught preservice teachers Theory and Application of Technology Integration.

When I first began teaching technology in public schools, I walked into a lab of mismatched Apple desktops, a dusty projector, and an interactive board that was still in the box from over a year prior to my arrival. Technology was not a high priority at the time. I gradually helped my school and district develop a successful technology integration plan that led to the first 1:1 school in the district before we went 1:1 district-wide. It makes me happy to know I have helped thousands of students prepare for their unknown future. This book is about my experiences with technology integration. I want to help other teachers integrate technology into their classrooms successfully, so they can learn from my failures, be so much further ahead of those learning it all on their own, and go on to have a positive impact on thousands of students.

Once upon a time, teachers thrived as the sage on the stage, and the great all-knowing source of information. These days are long gone. Educators that are willing to step outside of their comfort zone and give up some control are now the teachers that students gravitate to. They are the teachers that guide students to knowledge. This can be very scary and liberating at the same time but relieves pressure to have all the answers and empowers these future leaders of tomorrow to become independent thinkers and problem-solvers.

So how do you get there? I started by slowly taking advantage of the amazing resources technology can offer both teachers and students. It is unrealistic to expect teachers to take it all on at once. I believe it's a process by which you implement one thing at a time. If you fail, you make adjustments and try again. If you see success, feel the reward as an educator, and then have a deep desire to do more for both you and your students. Either way, it is an ongoing process.

Once you see the benefits of using this pedagogy, I believe you will never want to go back to the way education used to be.

Each chapter contains:

- Real-world scenarios of students so you know how to apply what you learned. These are real stories from my own classroom but names have been changed.

- Tech tools you can use in your classroom today to help you take advantage of technology resources. There should be no additional costs to you for software or services. Teachers are paid too little so taking advantage of free tools is of the utmost importance in education.

- Assignments for you to use the tool(s) or concepts covered in that chapter. Each assignment will become a part of an electronic portfolio or E-portfolio (eportfolio), that you will create using this book and potentially use to showcase your technology experience to future employers as you apply for teaching jobs.

- Numerous digital resources that accompany the content covered here within. For your convenience, these items have:

- QR codes if you are accessing this book via print
- Hyperlinks if you are accessing this book via digital PDF

All resources are available on my website at

https://www.teachandlearnwithtechnology.com/resources

Technology has changed our world and it has changed education. If we continue to teach students the way it has always been done, we are setting our students up for failure.

Our students need and deserve every opportunity for success. Our future depends on it.

Table of Contents

1 Motivation and Perspective Can Influence Success - *Teach and Learn with a Growth Mindset*

Michael is a social and bright young student in the fourth grade. When he bounces into my room he is quick to greet me with an energetic "Hello Mrs. Outka-Hill!" He loves coming to my Technology/STEM class once a week because he gets to use computers and robots. Michael has been fortunate to have both parents at home and extended family right here in his hometown. They are all very active in his life and try to attend as many events for him as possible. He participates in a variety of activities in and out of school. Anytime there is a school function, it is not uncommon to see his parents volunteering.

Michael's parents and family are quick to say "Michael is good at sports and he is so smart. Soccer and school come easy for him." This is mostly true as Michael is the captain of his team and his grades are consistently high.

Today in my class we are playing a problem-solving game on the computers. This game uses a ball and a set of ramps that when arranged appropriately, the ball falls into a bucket, a series of stars appear on the screen with a happy chime indicating success, and the student moves on to the next level. The game starts out easy. Michael and his partner are zipping through the levels and bragging to the students nearby about the level they are on. As the levels progress, Michael's facial expressions change from relaxed to stressed. As his eyebrows sink down and his lips tighten, I can see the tension start to build in his body. He now sits quieter and his partner solves the level they were stuck on so they move on. The next level is even harder yet and it's Michael's turn to run the computer mouse. His first attempt failed. This caused the ball to be stuck in the wrong spot in the game. His partner quickly says, "Michael, try to move that ramp over here", so Michael resets the game, moves the ramp and it is another failure. Now Michael is angry because he is not solving the game. His partner says "Let's try to move the ramp on the other side". Michael quickly moves the ramp and before his partner could make another suggestion he impatiently clicks on the ball to test it and the ball quickly gets stuck again. "I knew that wouldn't work!", Michael yells out. "I hate this game!", he shouts as he tosses the computer mouse away from him on the table, sulks back in his chair, and looks down with his arms crossed.

- Have you ever heard a student say, "I can't"?

- Have you seen a student fail at something and then either give up or maybe even cry?
- Do you view success as a choice?
- How do you view failure?

Take the Mindset Assessment

Available at https://www.teachandlearnwithtechnology.com/resources

Carol Dweck is a researcher and author that says students either have a "fixed mindset" or a "growth mindset". Although it may be difficult to decipher at first, the growth mindset student is more likely to continue to thrive through hardships and go on to achieve impressive results.

Students with a fixed mindset tend to have more anxiety and stress. They view intelligence, ability, and success are something you are born with and cannot be changed. When someone with a fixed mindset fails at something they believe it is because they are unable to do it and should never try it again. They believe they must settle with the hand

3

they are dealt with and that's it. These students tend to say words such as "I can't", "I'm dumb", or "I give up". Sometimes these students have been told by parents, teachers, or authoritative figures they are smart. This focuses on present attributes. These students will often avoid difficult things in fear of failure or demonstrating to others they are not as smart as they have been told.

Students with a growth mindset on the other hand believe intelligence, ability, and success are something you can work toward, improve and eventually even master if you continue to learn from previous mistakes. When someone with a growth mindset fails at something, they can learn from their failure, try again, and know what NOT to do next time, moving closer to success. They believe anything can be improved upon. These students tend to say words like "I can't YET", "I'm learning", or "I'll try". These students have likely been told they "are working hard" to focus on their efforts. They are more likely to try new things and continue to work on the things they want to be good at, regardless of what others think of them or have been told. Michael's partner clearly has more of a growth mindset and Michael has a more fixed mindset.

As an educator, what can you do to promote a growth mindset?

As the technology facilitator in my building, I teach pre-kindergarten through 6th-grade technology and STEM classes, but in collaboration with one tech aid, I am also responsible for all technology maintenance, inventory, repairs, and upkeep.

One morning I sat at my desk preparing for my first class when I received a phone call from a teacher.

"My interactive board isn't working and I really need it for this morning's lesson! Can you come to fix it?"

I had just a couple of minutes before my class arrived so I hurried to her classroom.

When I walked in the door, the teacher let out a loud sigh of relief and said 'I'm just terrible with technology. It just never goes right for me". She was obviously frustrated but relieved to see me there to fix it.

It took me a couple of minutes to determine the problem and make the necessary adjustments but it was up and running in a matter of minutes.

She shot me a brass "thank you" and followed it with "I may be calling you again soon. It probably won't last with my luck."

Start with YOU!

These comments, as innocent as they may seem, have an impact on the little ears listening in the room. Those students will not only believe technology never goes right but if my teacher can't keep her cool with technology, then how can I?

I suggest you start with yourself.

Think of how you would react to the following situations:

- When your computer (or any technology) isn't working the way you want or expect
- When the Internet is down
- When you don't know the answer to a question
- When a lesson doesn't go as planned
- When your school district implements a new curriculum, program, test, etc
- When you are faced with a difficult challenge.

What words do your students hear you saying? If you lose your patience, blame others or always take the easy route, your students will see this and replicate it. In contrast, a person with a growth mindset might say things like:

- "This isn't working as I expect. What can I/we try to do to fix it?"
- "Things might not be working as we expect, but I'm sure we can come up with something else that will work."
- "I don't know the answer to that. Let's learn it together."
- "That didn't work so let's try something else."
- "This is all new stuff to me too but I know we'll get it eventually."
- "This is hard but I will keep working at it until I get it."

I have seen how teachers that demonstrate a growth mindset become role models for their students. The students will see it's okay that things don't always go smoothly and perseverance will eventually lead to success.

Send growth mindset messages to your students.

As the teacher stands in front of the class giving directions, it appears as though Ian is not listening. He is looking around the room at the walls, the ceiling, the floor, out the window, at the loose string on his sweater, the new book on the shelf, and whatever else he finds interesting. He is very observant and ironically when it comes time to do the work, he completes it with no problem. Although he didn't make eye contact with the teacher, he was listening, while also taking in his surroundings.

Students DO notice and take in the things in their environment. When they are staring at the walls, I give them something to look at that sends the right messages. I believe most students are seeking mental stimulation, so giving them things to read and listen to that encourage them helps them receive positive and encouraging thoughts to ponder.

I hang posters in my classroom that encourage hard work and persistence.

 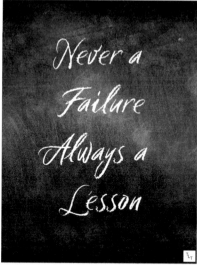

You can download these and other free resources at
https://www.teachandlearnwithtechnology.com/resources

Expect your students to succeed.

"Today I get to teach you all about the tiny and amazing city that makes up the inside of each computer. Everything has its own job and everything works together to get a job done." This is how I started teaching my 2nd graders about the hardware and software of a computer. This was a new computer science standard for me and although I could have started out by saying "Today we are going to learn about computer hardware and software", I chose to make it relatable and exciting. The sound of my voice and the expression on my face told students that this was going to be fun!

When the lesson is difficult or I am teaching something new, I find it helps me and the students when I get excited about it. I *expect* them all to learn it. Then, I challenge them to take it further than I presented it.

If I'm not excited about teaching it, they won't be excited about learning it.

Speak to students with growth mindset words:

"Lexie, you have been working so hard on this project! I have seen you try a couple of things and ask others for help and now you got it! I bet that feels good. What are you working on now?"

I enjoy praising students for their effort, practice, and perseverance. I use positive, specific feedback addressing exactly what they did correctly and where they could still improve, rather than a blanket statement like "good job".

I don't say a student is "smart", instead, I say, "you have worked so hard to get where you are", or a similar variation. This brings attention to their efforts rather than their ability.

Give students the opportunity to fail.

I stood over Andre's shoulder and watched him build his circuit with a battery, light bulb, and copper wire. I could see he was getting frustrated because the light wasn't coming on. I quickly noticed it was because the battery was backward. I could have told him this so he could move on but I chose to stand there and watch. He tried a couple of things, finally turned the battery over and the light came on. Literally and figuratively. He got it! The next time he made a circuit he was careful to align the positive and negative components correctly. If I had told him, I would have robbed him of the opportunity to solve the problem by himself and learn from his mistake.

Correcting a student before they have the opportunity to fail is like giving them the answers on a test. I let them do it wrong, allow time to consider alternative solutions, and opportunities to try again.

As a teacher, it is sometimes difficult to step back and watch a student do something I know won't work, but this is how they learn. No one learned to walk by watching someone else do it. We all learned by falling down and doing it again, over and over. This is what causes long-term memories and learning.

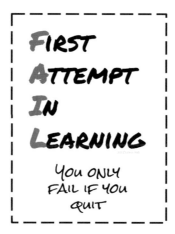

Image available at https://www.teachandlearnwithtechnology.com/resources

Ask LOTS of questions.

"Mrs. Outka-Hill, I want to record a sound for my project. Can I do that in this program?" When a student asks a question we often think we have to come up with a solution. I could have spent time exploring the features of the software to answer this student's question, but instead, I said" I don't know. Look into it and tell me what you find." It is such a relief to know I don't have to be an expert. By allowing students the opportunity to solve their own problems, I encourage them to do more thinking than I do. I have found the best way to do this is by answering their questions with another question. The fun part is I have learned things from my students by doing this. I encourage them to answer their own questions by responding with:

- What have you tried?
- Why do you think that didn't work?
- What else can you do?
- What do the directions say?
- Who have you asked?
- Where can you go for help?

Respond to struggling students with empathy and encouragement. Remember Michael? He was pouting in his chair about not knowing how to play the game. When a student says a fixed mindset statement, I can:

- respond with a question
- remind them of a time when they were successful
- give them alternate words to say

Sometimes when I get a new software program or new device, I choose a class to have "explore time" with it. I tell them it is new and I need them to find out what it does. We review expectations such as staying out of settings and being responsible with it, but then I let them discover the features and how to use them. It is so rewarding for them to teach me and their classmates something new while allowing them to uncover the use of these tools.

I knelt down next to Michael's chair so only he could hear me and I said "I see you're having a hard time with this level. This is a pretty hard game, but I know you can do hard things. Have you ever played this game before?"

"No", he snapped back to me.

"Then you don't know how to play it yet. This is like a 5-year-old playing a game of soccer. Were you as good at soccer when you were 5?"

"No", he smirked as if I was crazy.

"How many hours of soccer have you played?", I asked.

"I don't know, I've been playing forever", he answers.

"So you have a lot of practice?", I asked. He shrugs his shoulders and nods his head yes.

"Sounds like you need more practice with this game too. You just don't know how to play it yet". I slowly stand up and give him time to think about it. Before long I see him pointing to the screen and talking to his partner about the game again. It may not become his favorite game, but as long as he doesn't quit, it isn't a failure.

"The word "YET" can be used in so many ways to promote a growth mindset.

Available at https://www.teachandlearnwithtechnology.com/resources

Michael has been told his whole life he was "smart" and chances are, he has been successful at many things. Trying new things causes him to get frustrated when he doesn't immediately know it. He is also fearful of failure because that would mean he *wasn't* smart.

It will take time but using growth mindset words and showing him that failure is a GOOD thing and a natural part of learning will eventually get him to explore new opportunities. Some will be successful and some will not, but giving him the words to use and the actions to take give him a better chance at success now and in the future.

Watch this video about Growing Your Mind

Available at https://www.teachandlearnwithtechnology.com/resources

In the Classroom

For the past five years, I have started every school year teaching my students about mindset and the importance of allowing "failure" to teach them something. My students know how to respond to a classmate when they hear "I can't", they will answer back with the word "YET!".

I talk to my kindergarteners about how they learned to walk. They know they didn't just get up and walk away one day. Instead, they would fall down over and over again until they could run and jump without thinking about it.

Tech Tools

ClassDojo.com has a video series for young students about having a growth mindset and understanding the brain is like a muscle. The more you exercise (or challenge) that muscle, the more it will grow to be stronger for future challenges.

Older students need to know what a fixed and growth mindset looks like so they can help other students work toward a growth mindset. I like to give them alternate words to say to encourage a growth mindset in and out of my classroom.

Words for a Growth Mindset

Instead of:	Say:
I can't.	I will try
I'm done.	I can always make it better
This is too hard.	This may take some time.
I will never be smart	I can train my brain
I don't get it.	I don't get it YET.
I hate this. I'm not good at it.	This is hard for me but I'm learning from it.

Available at https://www.teachandlearnwithtechnology.com/resources

Goals

One way to encourage a growth mindset is to set goals. You can find all kinds of research and professional development about setting SMART goals for both teachers and students, but I have found a goal-setting technique that works well for anyone and seems to really hit home with what is important and doable.

Vision Boards

Vision boards are visual representations of things people hope to accomplish or have in life. I have found that when I have something to look at reminding me of where I want to go, I am more likely to make decisions based on achieving these things.

At the beginning of the semester, I have my college students make a vision board for the upcoming semester. I encourage you to complete the same assignment.

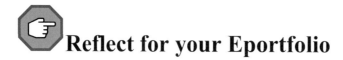 **Reflect for your Eportfolio**

You will make a vision board, but you need to narrow your attention first. A vision board is something that helps us stay focused on a specific goal or set of goals. It is composed of images that represent whatever you want to be, do or have in your life. Although we all have long-term goals, sometimes we need to focus on short-term goals to get us there. This vision board represents the goals you have for <u>THIS</u> year.

Answer the following questions.

Available at https://www.teachandlearnwithtechnology.com/resources

1. What have you always wanted to learn?

2. What hobbies, sports, or activities do you already do, but want to get better at doing?

3. Picture yourself at the end of the school year. What does it look like? What did you accomplish?

4. Where do you want to be after this semester?

5. What books do you want to read?

6. What problems do you want to solve?

7. What brings you joy?

8. How do you want your classmates to remember you? (smart, funny, athletic, caring, helpful, etc.)

9. Now choose at least 5 topics from the questions above that are more important than the others, to put on your vision board.

Write ONE word to represent each of the five things you chose. For example: if you always wanted to learn how to ski, you would write "ski".

1.

2.

3.

4.

5.

Let's take a look at a collage creation program and an app to complete this assignment. Although there are many available, I find these easy for young students to produce quality work, without getting distracted by the tool.

 Tech Tools

- Google Drawings - Google app used to create or edit shapes, photos, charts, and infographics. You will need to make a free Google account to access Google Drawings. We discuss more Google Apps in the next chapter.
- PicCollage app - Free app for creating photo collages and greeting cards from your images. This app can be loaded on any IOS or Android device. The free version will have a small watermark in the corner of each collage created.

WAIT! Don't start yet! Before copying images from the Internet, you need to understand copyright laws and fair-use images. *A picture is worth a thousand words* but it may cost you a thousand dollars or more if the picture is inappropriately used!

In the following video you will learn how to find images acceptable for use on Google. Keep in mind, Google may change its layout or functionality at any time, however, using appropriate images will remain a necessity. It is uber important for both you and your students to avoid breaking copyright laws.

 Watch this video about Creative Commons Image Citation

Available at https://www.teachandlearnwithtechnology.com/resources

Fair Use is the limited use of copyrighted material for your personal use without needing authorization from the owner.

 Tech Tools

You may also find Fair Use images at these sites:

- ■ Pics4Learning
- ■ FlickrCC
- ■ PhotosForClass
- ■ Pixabay.com
- ■ Pexels.com

There are many sites online that offer images. **Regardless of where you get them, you will still need to CITE your source with the URL of the page containing the image.** Place the URL below the image in the smallest font you can read.

https://commons.wikimedia.org/wiki/File:Red-eyed_Tree_Frog_(Agalychnis_callidryas)_1.png

See the example:

If you choose to use your own images, give yourself credit. YOUR work is also copyright material.

Google Drawing:

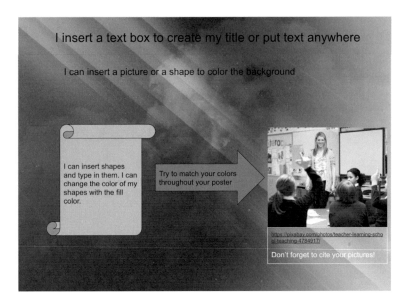

PicCollage App:

In the Classroom

Now that you know how to make a digital photo collage (your vision board) using either Google Drawing or the PicCollage app, think of ways your students could use this same tool to demonstrate understanding of content.

Here are some examples of student projects from pre-kindergarten to high school. There is no limit to age or content for photo collages and it can be a fun, project-based alternative for students to show what they know.

Sample Elementary Photo Collages:

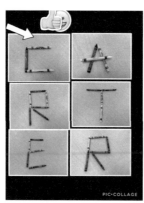

Spanish kindergarten class using a pencil to measure.

1st grade student spells his name

2nd grade learns about holidays

5th grade European Explorers

6th grade Civil War

Sample Secondary Photo Collage Topics:

US History

Branches of Government

Art/Photography

Architecture

Parts of _____

Foods high in protein

End of the year

Etc…

The options for creating a photo collage are endless and I have found many students would prefer to create a visual representation of their understanding than to write or type a paper about it. I like to understand what type of learners my students are, to help me decide what kind of assessments would most likely be successful. We will take a look at each type in chapter 3.

At the end of the project, I allow students to take a gallery walk. Students will work harder knowing they will have a broader audience than just the teacher and they will learn both content and creativity from each other.

☞ Reflect for your Eportfolio

Write a paragraph about the importance of a growth mindset and how you can encourage a growth mindset in both you and your students in your classroom. You will use this reflection along with your vision board later in your eportfolio.

We will be discussing what an eportfolio is, what should be included within it, and why every teacher should have one as we continue through this book.

2 Do More Than "Google it"! - Teach and Learn with Google Apps

Brenden is a high school history teacher. He has tried numerous word processors in the past depending on what his colleagues are using. Now he has files on his desktop at school and on a seven-year-old laptop at home. He needs to upgrade to a new laptop but just the thought of moving files or worse yet, LOSING files makes him fearful. He would also need to upgrade to a newer version of his current word processor to be compatible with a new device. This just isn't in his budget as a second-year teacher. He also finds himself attaching draft documents to emails and when his colleagues return them in an email, he doesn't know what was changed, not to mention the numerous versions he ends up with scattered on various computers.

Does this sound like you? Choosing applications that are not only appropriate for both teachers and students but also affordable can be challenging.

Google Apps

Unless you have been living under a rock for the past two decades, you know Google for its search engine capabilities. If you don't know something, you can just "Google it". But Google also has a collection of apps that provide a simple and FREE solution to file creation, file organization, and file sharing for both teachers and students. Every teacher knows how important free resources are! You can create an account at https://www.google.com/account/about/

Your school or district may already have a Google for Education account. This gives teachers and students access to additional apps focused toward education and allows your IT department to enable or disable features for either teachers or students and monitor things appropriately. This is also free at https://edu.google.com/ .

Google Drive

Google Drive is a cloud-based storage place for not only all the Google files I have, but it can store any file for easy access from any device connected to the Internet. If you have registered for a free account you can access your drive at https://drive.google.com/ .

Here's how it works: Brenden has files on multiple computers. He can drag them into the Google Drive window or use the upload button to save it to Drive. Now he can access these files from any computer or mobile device connected to the Internet and he no longer has files covering his desktop. One place stores them all. Even if they aren't Google files. He can store any word-processing document, spreadsheet, slideshow, image, video, audio, or even proprietary files.

I encourage both teachers and students to store their files on Google Drive because after working in IT for numerous years I have learned it is rare for a computer to give you any warning before it crashes. Recovering files on a crashed device is difficult to retrieve and sometimes can't be done. Storing them on Google Drive means they are safe from getting lost.

Google Docs

Google Docs https://docs.google.com/ is a word-processing application that does so much more. It has all of the basic editing and formatting features, I can insert images, charts, and tables, and it keeps a complete history of everything I have done so I can view or restore it to any version. But what sets Google Docs apart from desktop publishers is:

- All changes are saved in real-time (no more forgetting to save before the power goes out)
- Works seamlessly with other Google Apps
- Other word processing documents can be opened and edited in Google Docs
- Documents can be shared with others to view, comment or edit
- Collaborators can all work on the document in real-time
- A history of all edits and their editors is kept for each document

Reflect for your Eportfolio

What program did you type your reflection paragraph in for the previous chapter? Was it Google Docs? If not, I suggest you drag the file you created into your Google Drive or click the "+New" button at the top left and upload your file.

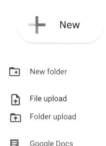

You can now open your file and edit it with Google Docs, even if that isn't the program you created it in. As long as you have Internet access, you can view, edit, and share this file. You can also create a new Google Doc from the +New drop-down.

As you go through this book, you will be preparing an eportfolio to better market yourself as a teacher and show off what you know, have done, and can do to potential employers. As you continue through this book and come across the "Reflect for your Eportfolio" sections, I encourage you to use Google Apps to keep it all in one location. You will be making your final Eportfolio using another Google App and like it or not - Google likes Google stuff. Keeping it all on one platform will make it easier for you in the end. TRUST ME on this one!

Brenden can open his existing word-processing documents in Google Docs and share them with his colleagues. As others make changes to the document, he will be able to see the changes, comment on them and review the history of all changes as well as who made them. No more time-consuming email attachments and saving multiple versions!

In the Classroom

Students are able to open a Google Doc and take notes, collaborate with a partner in real-time, at school or at home, and create organized documents using spelling, grammar, and formatting tools.

Students can share their documents with the teacher and comments can be left for the student throughout. If multiple students work on an assignment, the teacher can check the history and see what student contributed to what part. Everything is time-stamped and saved in Google Drive.

Google Slides

Google Slides https://slides.google.com/ is a slideshow application. Just like Google Docs, Slides integrates seamlessly with other Google apps. Most people are aware of how a slideshow is used to present material, but teachers can also use Google Slides to create posters, certificates, interactive documents, collaborative documents for their class, and more. Let's look at some examples:

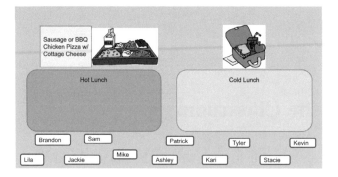

Click and drag - student attendance

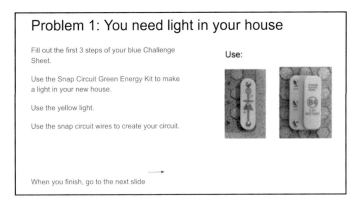

Directions to be shared digitally or printed out

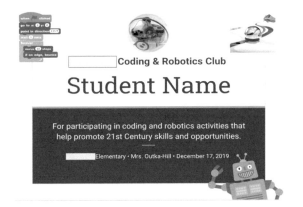

Reproducible certificates

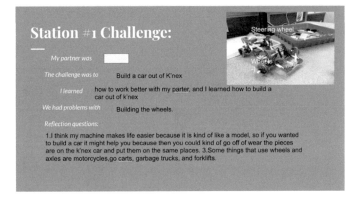

Student reflection journals

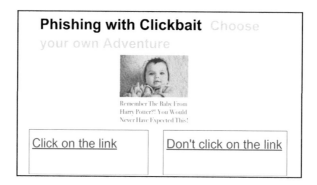

Choose your own adventure with hyperlinks

Draggable assessments

AND SO MUCH MORE!

Here are some basic slideshow tips I like to use when creating presentations:

1. Keep it simple

2. Add color

3. Use transitions and animations sparingly, but when appropriate

4. Use high quality graphics

This slideshow with additional slides and tips is available at
https://www.teachandlearnwithtechnology.com/resources

Please don't be a "death by slideshow" teacher! Be creative when presenting information and don't feel like you need to be the all-knowing expert. It's okay for students to learn things on their own.

In the Classroom

My students like to use Google slides as well. Not for presentations but they can create projects easier than on a document because shapes, images, and text boxes are easy to manipulate.

They also use Google Slides when they complete reflection journals at the end of the day or at the end of a project.

I have had some students tell me they like to use Google Slides to take notes. This way they can separate content and import images (along with the URL). They like the drag-and-drop features of placing content anywhere on the page without having to format it the way word processors do. It's easier for them to make sense of later.

 **Google Sheets**

Google Sheets http://sheets.google.com/ is a spreadsheet application that has most of the functions of other spreadsheets, but it has the collaborative and sharing abilities of other Google Apps.

Teachers have LOTS of data to keep organized! From student rosters and grades to their own daily, weekly, and yearly planning. Sheets are a great way to stay organized and the formatting makes them look less like a spreadsheet and more like a chart.

Here is my lesson plan template:

A1	fx					
	A	B	C	D	E	F
1		Monday	Tuesday	Wednesday	Thursday	Friday
2	8:40-8:45					
3	8:45-9:40	3A (8:55-9:40)	4A		5A	6A
4						
5	Reflect					
6	8:50-9:30			KB		
7						
8	Reflect					
9	9:35-10:15			KC		
10						
11	Reflect					
12	10:20-11:00			KA		
13						
14	Reflect					
15	10:00-11:00	4B	4C		5B	5C
16						
17	Reflect					
18	11:00-11:40	planning	planning	planning	planning	planning
19						
20	11:40-12:15	duty/lunch	duty/lunch	duty/lunch	duty/lunch	duty/lunch
21				District meetings		
22	12:55-1:55				6B	6C
23						
24	Reflect					
25	2:00 - 2:45	1B	1C			1A/2A
26						
27	Reflect					
28	2:45-3:30	3B	3C		2B	2C
29						
30	Reflect					
31						
32						

+ ≡ 3 ▾ 11/22-26 ▾ 11/15-19 ▾ 11/8-12 ▾ 11/1-5 ▾ 10/25-29 ▾ 10/18-22 ▾ 10/11-15 ▾ 10/4

Download this template for free at
https://www.teachandlearnwithtechnology.com/resources

Each year it varies but the overall layout stays the same. I allow for planning space and reflection space. Notice the tabs at the bottom for each week so I can use the same document all year long.

In the Classroom

I like my students to discover spreadsheets at an early age to learn vocabulary words such as cell, row, and column. This helps them later when they learn graphing skills.

My third graders love to do Pixel art around the holidays. This is where a cell has conditional formatting to change a specific color depending on the number they type in the cell.

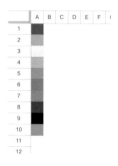

Download a template for free at
https://www.teachandlearnwithtechnology.com/resources

This is a great opportunity for them to learn spreadsheets without the complicated functions that come when they get older. However, my older students are excited when I tell them about all the math it can do for them.

 Google Forms

In my world, Google Forms http://forms.google.com/ is a teacher's best friend! I can create assessments that are easily shared with students and are graded automatically. Google forms can also be used for parent sign-ups, staff polls, and anywhere I need to collect data.

All form results are displayed nicely in summary or individual format with colorful charts and they can all be exported into a spreadsheet for manipulation with formulas and functions. Questions and answers can include text, images, and videos. Question types can be multiple choice, checkbox, short or long answer, file upload, and more.

Google Forms collect any data that is time-stamped upon submission.

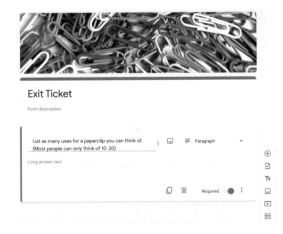

I also like to use Google forms for exit tickets.

Google Classroom

Google Classroom https://classroom.google.com/ is Google's version of a Learning Management System (LMS). These are used for a virtual classroom environment for teachers to share content and assignments with students and students can complete the work, turn it in and see their grades online. It is a controlled environment where teachers can communicate with their students and parents can see their child's work and communicate with the teacher all in one place.

Google Classroom integrates all Google Apps as well as any outside link into a feed format for students to access at any time from a device connected to the Internet. The calendar helps students keep on top of due dates and the communication between students can be opened, closed, or monitored by the teacher, providing a place to practice safe digital communication skills.

Google Drawings

Google Drawings https://drawings.google.com/ was covered in great detail in chapter one. Google Drawings is an app that allows you to combine images, shapes, symbols, and text to create posters, charts, or any graphic design you need. I can download images as jpeg, png, pdf, or vector files that can be used anywhere.

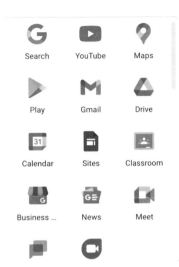 Google has a number of other apps in its G Suite for Education but the apps listed above are the apps I most frequently use. Most importantly, they are all Internet-based and free. Additional Google apps will be covered in other chapters.

Reflect for your Eportfolio

1. Create a free Google account, if you haven't already.
2. Create a new Google Doc and type a summary of how Google Apps can benefit your classroom.
3. Give one specific example of how you could use any of the Google Apps listed in this chapter in your classroom.

3 Encouraging Students to go Fishing - *Teach and Learn with Current Theories*

Angelica is like many students, she participates in class, is friendly, and seems to understand the content, but when it comes time to take the test, she seems to freeze up. Although it appears that she knows the content, she just can't demonstrate her knowledge on the test. This can happen for a couple of reasons:

- She gets nervous and her test anxiety doesn't allow her brain to think clearly.
- The test timing, location, or format doesn't allow for a clear depiction of her understanding.
- She has been taught to memorize and regurgitate information but doesn't clearly understand how the content connects to the real world.
- Maybe she didn't actually understand the content as it appears.

- Or it could be a combination of these things.

There has been a long debate about how to get a clear understanding of what goes on in each student's brain, whether they comprehend the content, and whether testing is an accurate demonstration of this knowledge. Although we can attempt to butt heads with the education system and its beliefs on testing, testing will likely continue until we have a better way of seeing what goes on inside our students' heads. However, I like to provide an opportunity for students to apply their knowledge in a variety of ways. It could be on a test, a paper, a project, or in a real life setting through current teaching methods.

What is the job of a teacher?

This question may seem simple at first glance. A teacher's job is to teach. Right? WRONG! *What?* Let's dive deeper:

- ➤ WHY does a teacher teach?
  - ○ So students can learn.
- ➤ Why do students need to learn?
  - ○ So they can understand the content taught.
- ➤ Why do they need to understand the content taught?
  - ○ So they can apply it to their life.
- ➤ Why do students need to apply content in their life?
  - ○ So they can be successful later in life.

➢ What does success look like later in life?

○ Thriving, independent, stable, and productive citizens within a community.

So, I will ask the question again. What is a teacher's job?

To teach students how to be thriving, independent, stable, and productive citizens within a community.

Does that mean they need to know and understand math? Probably. Do they need to read and write? Most likely. Do they need to memorize the periodic table? Maybe. But realistically, very few will need this skill.

The education system was founded on the ideals of the Industrial Revolution. People became factory workers with a basic set of skills and knowledge, otherwise known as the three Rs (reading, writing, and arithmetic). Those that understood reading, writing, and math excelled to the top and this continued for decades. Today, many of these skills are no longer the focus of employment in our society. Now before I have math and ELA teachers hunting me down, I am not discounting the validity of these subjects. These are very much needed and often assumed when hiring! Employers are now looking at how someone can *apply* these skills in a technical environment.

Let's take a look at some ways this can be done.

The Sage On the Stage versus the Guide on the Side

Thinking back to your K-12 school experience, many of your teachers probably resembled the "sage on the stage". These teachers stood in front of the class downloading their knowledge onto the students while the students gazed authoritatively up at their wise and all-knowing teacher. Students were expected to sit in rows facing the board so they could take in every word the teacher said or wrote down. The only sound expected from students was the scratching of notes or the awes of amazement. This scenario puts pressure on the teacher to know everything and have complete control over every movement and sound twenty-five-ish students make. This is not only an unrealistic expectation but it's uncomfortable for everyone in the room, students and teachers alike. When the teacher didn't want to lecture, he or she would turn to the textbook and assign reading on the topic, assuming students will have a complete understanding after reading it. To test their understanding, students would answer the questions at the end of the chapter, and complete a worksheet or other homework assignment.

If students like Angelica are placed in a class like this, there is no relationship building that occurs between her and the teacher and certainly, no independent thought is occurring. When she doesn't do well on the test, often her teacher doesn't know why or what to do to help her other than present the material all over again, because she must not have got it the first time.

What can change to help both Angelica and the teacher?

Jordan is Angelica's math teacher and she prides herself on understanding her content area. She is very knowledgeable and has been in teaching long enough to attend conferences, read books, meet people, and create a curriculum full of deep and wonderful information. This is great, but can she pour her knowledge into her students so they are as passionate about the content as she is? Probably not. The reason she is passionate is that she was allowed to pursue her interests and she did it willingly and excitedly. No one can make anyone do anything. Ever. Just try telling a four-year-old to sit still, or a seventeen-year-old to sit still, or even a sixty-year-old because

1. No one wants to be told what to do and

2. People want to think for themselves.

So how can we TEACH someone then? I like to allow them to learn it. When I provide the right environment to explore, experiment, fail, and extend a student's interest as far as they choose to go, I will often be surprised by what students can learn.

When Angelica comes to my class, she likes to tell me what she did over the weekend while she works on her assignment. She tells me she likes to read but doesn't have many books at home. She says she has three younger siblings and spends the weekends alternating between Mom's house and Dad's. She likes Origami and brings some into class to show me. Even if I have seen a similar one, or think I know more, I always let her do the talking while I just listen. I make sure to be enthusiastic about each creation. I stop what I'm doing, sit down next to her, ask her how she made it, what she likes about it, and what was hard about it. Angelica says she wants to make an owl because her grandma likes owls. I ask her to show it to me when she gets it done and thank her saying "I can't wait to see it"! This is called building a relationship. This is what connects people together and without it, the conversation has a performer and an audience rather than a give-and-take interconnection.

Once I have a relationship with my students I can help them teach themselves. Rather than pouring my knowledge out for the students to absorb, I can start by asking questions and letting students share what they already know.

My kindergarten class comes into the room and I greet them with "hello, it's great to see you today" and "that new haircut looks great on you". They sit down and I tell them we are using robots to learn about counting. I get two or three hands that shoot up blurting out "I have a robot at home". As a teacher, I have the choice to tell them to quiet down and I will tell them all about robots or I can say "Really? That's great! How does a robot work? Do you talk to it or give it commands? What happens if you give it the wrong command? How do you tell a robot to do the same thing over and over without having to give it each command? What happens if you leave your robot on overnight?" By asking these questions, my students can become the teachers and they can share how to give coding commands, use a repeat loop, and turn the robot off when they finish. It's my guiding questions that keep the conversation on topic.

When I give students the opportunity to teach others, predict, hypothesize, research, and explore, they often retain the information much more. It goes back to the old saying "Give a man a fish and you feed him for a day. Teach a man how to fish and feed him for a lifetime."

Allow your students to go fishing!

I have seen the result of teachers stepping to the side and guiding their students toward something and allowing the students to lead the way. The students feel a sense of independence and accomplishment. If they start to veer off a little, some gentle guidance from the teacher can steer them back in the right direction.

Don't be a sage on the stage - be a guide at the side.

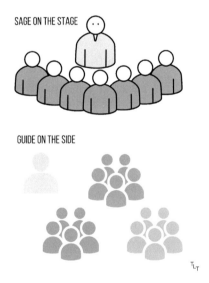

Available at https://www.teachandlearnwithtechnology.com/resources

A guide on the side no longer has to be the expert and THIS IS OKAY. This is a hard concept at first because so many teachers are used to having to be the expert. I have found the best way to move from being a traditional teacher to becoming more of a facilitator is to allow the students to do more, giving them ownership of their learning. Facilitators are people that allow movement and conversations to occur about a specific topic and gently redirect those that get off-topic. It is sometimes helpful to physically move away from the front of the room. I have gone as far as not even having a front or back of the room. This can be scary at first because now the students are leading the way, but it can be very exciting for both the students and the teacher BECAUSE the students are leading the way. Facilitators ask lots of questions. When a student asks a question, I try to respond with another question.

Let's go back to my kindergarten class learning about robotics. I asked lots of questions and those that knew the answers became the teachers. Those that didn't know the answers now have someone else to go to for help. This builds a classroom community and allows everyone to be an expert at something. Later in class when a student asks me what to do, my response can be:

- What have you tried?
- Where can you go for directions?
- Who have you asked?

If this sounds familiar, it is because being a facilitator encourages a growth mindset (from chapter 1). It gives them the confidence to try new things and be proud of their successes because they earned them.

If you were to walk past my room, you would hear lots of noise. Quiet doesn't necessarily mean learning is happening. My students are allowed to talk, move around the room, ask students questions, and get excited about their successes. Conversations should be on-topic and movements need to be safe. If I think conversations are off-topic I simply ask a question such as "What's the next step?", to get them right back on task.

Being a facilitator doesn't discount a teacher's knowledge. I can still share a wealth of information but only once a student is ready and requests it. When a student doesn't know where to go next, when they don't understand why something happens or they need an explanation, then they come to me or the textbook or other resource to find the answer. This means they are pursuing the knowledge and WANT to know the answer versus being told they will need to know something. It has become their choice.

Flipped Classroom

Think back to your K-12 education again. During a typical class time, where was the teacher when they were "teaching"? Where were the students when they were "learning"?

If your teachers stood at the front of the room while students sat at their desks facing the front of the room (a sage on the stage), this was a teacher-centered classroom.

There are times teachers need students to know something before they can move on. Your teacher may have given you information either in the form of a lecture, reading a text, or doing research. When did this usually occur? In class, right? Then you took the homework home with you to practice the content. But wait! When is the teacher most valuable? We know many students don't have people at home to help them with homework. The homework is often where the teacher is needed the most. Students can be reading, listening to lectures, or researching on their own time, so when they come to class, they already know what they don't know. This is called a flipped classroom.

A **flipped classroom** is when students prepare outside of class by reading, listening to audio recordings, watching videos, or doing topic-specific research on their own. When they come to class they will demonstrate their learning with the teacher present and have the help of the teacher to clarify misconceptions. This is a student-centered classroom. With the help of technology, this is easier than ever before. Students can listen to or watch everything on their phones before class or if they are at the elementary level, they can visit a listening center before doing the work. In this way, teachers are able to clone themselves to other places while attending to the things that matter most. We will discuss the ways to do this in future chapters.

VARK Model

Angelica loves to work with her hands. She understands by seeing things. Her Origami becomes a structure that connects to her understanding of the real world. Although she says she likes to read, she doesn't read often and it is not her first choice of things to do. When a teacher lectures (auditory) or assigns a chapter in a book (read/write), Angelica is not excited about doing the work and may not be learning to her potential. Most assessments are given in a read/write format which again is not her preference.

We all have preferences in how we learn. According to Neil

Fleming's VARK Model, there are 4 types of learners.

- **Visual** (images, diagrams, videos)
- **Auditory** (lectures, discussions, music)
- **Reading/Writing** (reading text, writing text)
- **Kinesthetic** (hands-on experiments, movement, tactile exploration)

Neil Fleming introduced the VARK Model in 1987. People tend to gravitate toward one or two of these learning types.

What type of learner are you?

Let's imagine you were a kindergartener in my class learning about robots. Would you prefer to:

1. Watch someone demonstrate how robots work.
2. Listen to someone tell you how robots work.
3. Read about how robots work and then take notes on what you read.
4. Get a robot and try different things to get it to work.

You may not know which one you prefer most but you will usually know which learning styles you don't like. Every student is different in their learning style. With the help of technology, all students can be given the opportunity to learn in their preferred learning style.

In the Classroom

Knowing every student learns differently, how can you present material that reaches all student learning types?

- Presenting material in all methods rather than just one will assure all students will benefit. This could be including all learning styles in one presentation or presenting four types in each style.
- Providing students with a variety of content to learn from and then giving students a choice of how to learn the content. They will enjoy the choice to own their learning and will likely learn more by choosing their learning style. They may even choose two styles which means they are getting the information twice.

Let's go back to Angelica. She may have a different learning style than the way the information was presented, but she may also need the opportunity to apply her new knowledge in a way she won't forget. She will likely remember something she does rather than something she heard or read about because she likes to use her hands.

4 Cs

In 1970, the Top 5 Most Valuable Skills, in order of importance, according to The Fortune 500 were:

1. Writing
2. Computation

3. Reading

4. Oral communication

5. Listening

(Darling-Hammond, 2013)

These were skills people needed to be successful in the job market. As technology changed society and rote memorization became less important (thank you Google and Siri), the skills of employees changed as well.

In 2002 The National Education Association (NEA) developed the Framework for 21st Century Learning which encompasses the 4 C's. These were skills identified as being valuable in the classroom and for success in the real world after graduation. These were:

- Critical Thinking and Problem-Solving
- Communication
- Collaboration
- Creativity and Innovation

Poster available at https://www.teachandlearnwithtechnology.com/resources

Why are these Cs so important?

In 2020, the top skills employers were looking for were identified as being both hard skills and soft skills. (Anderson, 2020)

Soft Skills:	Hard skills:
1. Creativity	1. Blockchain
2. Persuasion	2. Cloud Computing
3. Collaboration	3. Analytical
4. Reasoning	4. Artificial
5. Adaptability Intelligence	5. UX Design
6. Emotional Intelligence	

When a kindergartener begins school, we have no way of knowing what the hard skills will look like in thirteen years, but regardless of how they change, the 4 Cs remain fairly consistent and can help students grow and evolve to meet those both hard and soft skills to be successful when they get there.

If we teach today's students like we taught yesterday's, we rob them of tomorrow. ~John Dewey

A sage on the stage doesn't allow for any of the Cs to occur and most importantly, deprives the class of the teacher-student and student-student relationships.

Real world experiences have included these 4 Cs since the early days of man. Providing real world problems encourages critical thinking and problem solving skills. Word problems in math are a great way to do this but making sure the students can relate to the problems is essential. In any subject, you can include classroom, playground, or other school settings with specific teacher and student names. Allow them to act out each scenario to see each component and analyze possible solutions.

More recently, students are not only encouraged to problem solve but also to problem-find. As students begin seeing problems and generate possible solutions, they are taught to think critically and develop empathy for others in the world.

 **In the Classroom**

The hard skills listed above are very specific, so let's instead focus on the soft skills. The 4 Cs include collaboration, communication, critical thinking, and creativity.

The act of critical thinking is based on evaluating and applying knowledge that helps prepare students for solving complex problems.

Every decision students make helps to foster critical thinking skills. The best way for a teacher to encourage decision making is to ask questions and allow students to discover the consequences of their choice. Critical thinkers tend to be great problem solvers. Critical thinkers are often creative in their solutions while also having persistence and patience. Encouraging a growth mindset can also help to develop strong critical thinkers.

A classroom based on the 4 Cs requires a shift from a teacher-centered to a student-centered classroom. Consider changing student desks from rows to groups, allowing students to help each other and even work together on specific assignments. This moves the attention away from the teacher. When students work together, they will consider things they would not have thought of otherwise. Communication and collaboration are often lumped together but don't need to be. I tell my students communicating means to listen just as much as it means to talk. Collaborating means working together toward a common goal, making sure everyone participates and considers the opinions of all members involved. Although students are working together and can ask for help, they are not allowed to give another student an answer but instead can point, explain, or guide another student through a problem. Rather than "what" questions, students are encouraged to ask "how", "where", and "why" questions.

To help facilitate communication and collaboration between students, I have a poster of the 4 Cs and another poster that says "Ask 3 Before Me". This way, when a student asks me for help, I can reply with "Who else have you asked"? Most of the time they will find someone else that knows how to help them. In the rare instance they have already asked then I can interject with my questions and then point them in the direction of their answer.

Elementary and secondary posters are available at
https://www.teachandlearnwithtechnology.com/resources

As students get older, their communication and collaboration is encouraged to branch outside of their friends and to embrace technology sources. They may find videos made by experts in the field. Blogs and chat boards can hold discussions about their topic or they can email a professional in their community. With the rise in video, our world is getting more comfortable with jumping onto a Zoom call and not only hearing but seeing the experience. This opens doors for students to communicate and collaborate with other students and professionals in virtually every content area.

Many teachers have dedicated a corner of their room to a makerspace. A **makerspace** is a collection of materials where students can explore, build and provide learning experiences where creativity can flourish. These materials can range from inexpensive cardboard and food packages to commercial made building blocks, craft materials and kits.

When combined with technology, students can design in a digital environment and then create a conceptual product that reflects their ideas. Even my third grade students are learning to design on a Computer Aided Design program or CAD program and then 3D print their creations. As students get older they learn to embrace their ideas and capitalize on their creations or use them to solve real-world problems. I have a third grade student that goes to the mountains with family friends. One of those friends has limited functionality of his lower limbs and is confined to a wheelchair. My student helped design and 3D print a paddle attachment for the steering wheel of a side-by-side ATV so this man can operate it with his hands. This is real world problem solving at its finest!

As a teacher, consider coming up with open-ended questions that have more than one correct answer or even better, allow students to come up with their own problems. Ask questions that are not "Google-able" to encourage the student to come up with something original. If they have a close connection to it, they are more likely to be invested and remember it. Allowing creativity means students can demonstrate their understanding in whatever way they choose. This will often depend on their learning style and of course, their personal choice.

Oftentimes the 4 Cs are used in conjunction with each other, but each has its importance in preparing students for their future. There is no limit to the possibilities when you allow your students the freedom to learn and use the 4 Cs.

3 Additional Cs

The above 4 Cs are soft skills students should practice daily to be more successful in school and in life. I propose 3 additional Cs that the teacher can do to be a better facilitator and nurture a thriving classroom: **choice**, **curiosity** and **caring**.

If you give a student a red marker, they will inevitably want a different color because they feel they have no choice in the matter. If you hold out a red and blue marker and give them the choice between the two, they feel empowered. Even adults prefer to have choices. When students are young, choices are best left between two or three items, rather than the entire bucket until their decision making skills have matured. Making choices is what life is all about so allowing students to practice this skill can help them be more prepared to make more difficult decisions later in life.

A facilitator answers questions with questions and sparks a student's curiosity. This curiosity can lead a student down a path that allows them to explore options or relates to their experiences that the teacher would never have considered. Allowing students to get curious about the content means they are making personal connections and is more meaningful to them.

The 3rd C is caring. I mentioned the importance of building relationships with your students earlier in this chapter. Most teachers are in the profession because they have the biggest hearts and genuinely want the best for their students. We sometimes get in a hurry to meet our own deadlines but please remember you are shaping little lives and teaching them how to treat others. Once you ask them a question, simply taking the time to listen is one of the best ways to show you care.

It is easy to look at our students' test scores and judge whether you and they are on pace for the year. All students, regardless of their future endeavors, will be more successful if they can think creatively, collaborate with others, communicate, and produce something creative. By implementing choice, curiosity, and caring into your classroom, it will be more enjoyable and your students will have one more advantage over those who come from anything less than a student centered classroom. I will refer to the 4 Cs again many times throughout this book.

Project Based Learning

Project based learning or PBL is giving students the opportunity to actively solve real world problems with projects. It combines the 4 Cs with real world situations where students can demonstrate their understanding with voice and choice. The famous revised version of Bloom's Taxonomy (Bloom, et. al., 2001) has creativity as the sixth and final stage at the top of the pyramid. This is where students build something tangible to demonstrate full understanding. Allowing students to be creative can be a fun way to learn and assess content. This is at the core of PBL.

When technology is combined with PBL, students can be a problem-finder, research information, communicate and collaborate with others outside of the school, and make a difference by solving the problem in a creative way. It also allows for the presentation of material in a way that could otherwise not be done.

3 Es

Remember Angelica's math teacher, Jordan? Jordan likes to use a lot of PowerPoint presentations in her class. This way she can show the text as well as images, charts, or graphs. She is confident in her technology use because she has used presentations for many years. She has learned to make colorful templates that match the holidays and she even uses transitions between slides. She will often use an online quiz to assess her students in ways other than paper and pencil. Is this the best way to present information to her students like Angelica?

If you are like most teachers when it comes time to find a technology tool you head to the Internet. When you enter a search such as "technology tools" you will be inundated with a number of new and old tools that may or may not be appropriate for your needs. Please don't feel like you need to use every tool! And although a tool may work for your colleagues, it might be the wrong tool for you or your students. If you get nothing else out of this book, I want you to remember one thing:

 It is not about the tech tool, it is about student learning.

As a teacher, you may have a donation from your PTO, your department purchased a new tech tool last year or you have funds allocated for a specific technology. These can be great and wonderful things, but I caution you about the pressure to use such tools. When you begin with the tool, your focus is no longer on student achievement. No standard anywhere will say students need to operate a piece of technology. Technology becomes a gateway for a better understanding of learning content standards.

Always start with the learning goal in mind.

When you consider using a technology tool, you need to decide if it will help your students achieve their learning goals. **The Triple E Framework** was developed by prof Liz Kolb at the University of Michigan in 2011(Kolb, 2020). This model helps teachers determine if the technology will help students:

- Engage
- Enhance
- Extend

Engagement is where the technology helps the students stay focused on the lesson and the content while not being distracting. Technology should be an afterthought for students. If they are spending more time on the uniqueness of the technology and not focusing on the content, then the technology tool may not be the right one. Students should be actively participating in a lesson while their thoughts are on the content and the technology helps them understand it better.

Enhancement is where the technology adds significant value to the lesson and allows students to do something they couldn't otherwise do. If the technology is simply a replacement for existing classroom tools, then maybe the classroom tools would be a better choice. Technology should give students the opportunity to learn in a way they could not learn without it.

Extension is where the technology takes an existing lesson beyond what could happen without it. This is where technology becomes the tool that connects learning with the real world. If technology keeps students isolated to the school, classroom, or to themselves, then maybe something else would be more helpful in bridging the gap. Technology can connect students with people, opportunities, locations, or skills outside of the classroom so they understand why the content is relevant to the world.

The https://www.tripleeframework.com/ website

has free resources for teachers to help them discern whether the technology provides value to their students' learning. The Triple E Evaluation Rubric is an online tool that gives you a number score between 0 and 18 signifying a good tool, an average tool, or a poor tool.

3 Additional Es

There is great value in the research Professor Kolb had done based on the Triple E Framework, but I feel there is a piece missing. Of course, education is about our students, but what about us, the teacher? Over the past few years, I have come to the conclusion that there are three more Es to this framework. The first three Es developed by Professor Kolb are about student impact, but the teacher that implements this tool also needs consideration. So I propose three additional E's or the Triple E Framework X2.

The 1st E is **efficient**. Does this tool help the teacher save time or energy for lesson preparation, assessment, grading, recording, or analyzing data? Many tools take some time to set up initially but end up saving time on the back end. This can also allow for more time to be spent on other things like making connections and addressing student needs.

The 2nd is **effective**. Does the tool do what I want it to do? We can get caught up in the newest technology or what is shiny right now, but does it help students learn, does it help you teach, and does it help seamlessly collect, store and analyze data? Some tools are too complicated with too many pieces that can divert from this. I make sure I have a goal for all technology tools and it meets that goal.

The 3rd E is **economical**. Some companies waived their fees for the first month or a short period of time. We all know teachers are not overpaid and choosing free tools is a no-brainer. Even the tools with free trials will someday come to an end and the time and effort I put into those tools will either be lost or I will be forced to pay the fee. Subscriptions can be dangerous territory as well. My school or my budget may be able to afford a tool for one year but due to common budget cuts, they will not be able to maintain the cost over several years. That money quickly adds up!

When objectively considering either new technology or even analyzing new technology tools, I like to use the Triple E Framework X2 combining Kolb's Engage, Enhance and Extend for student benefit with Efficient, Effective, and Economical for teacher benefit to make sure each tool is worth using.

think

Let's think about Jordan's use of Powerpoint presentations in her class. Is this a good use of technology according to the Triple E Framework?

Generally, PowerPoint (or Google Slides or any slideshow) is not the best way to keep students engaged in the lesson. They can easily focus their attention elsewhere without a teacher knowing.

I have found that PowerPoint is not designed to enhance the lesson for the students but instead, to make the presentation of information easier for the teacher. To truly provide value to the students, it needs to meet students at different levels, and provide students with opportunities to create, interact, or provide a better understanding of the content than traditional instruction can provide.

Generally, Powerpoint does not extend the lesson in a way that connects the students with the real world outside of their class or allows students to build their own skills.

SAMR

Let's discuss another method that helps guide teachers to appropriate technology integration in their classroom. From the previous PowerPoint example, it is clear that just because technology is being used in the classroom, doesn't mean it is to the benefit of the students, specifically if it is teacher use. In chapter 2, we covered numerous Google Apps. Let's consider students' use of a word processor. I have often seen teachers require students to type up final drafts of reports or assignments on a word processor such as Google Docs or MS Word. From a teacher's perspective, typing may keep students engaged, it enhances the outcome to be a formatted and printed document versus a hand-written document. And the topic may be about something outside of class that connects students to the real world, but is this the best use of technology integration?

Ruben Puentedura developed the SAMR Model in 2010 (Puentedura, 2010) that categorizes technology integration into 4 levels:

- Substitution
- Augmentation
- Modification
- Redefinition

Substitution is when a technology tool is a direct replacement of an existing, non-technical, classroom instructional tool such as paper and pencil.

Augmentation is also a replacement for a non-technical tool but has functional improvement.

Modification is when the lesson looks completely different than it would look without the use of technology and students gain a better understanding.

Redefinition is when students are allowed to do something very different from the original lesson and they could not do it without the use of technology.

Let's consider word processors as our technology and view use at each level:

- Substitution - a student types a paper instead of writing it
- Augmentation - a student types a paper using spell check, and grammar check. Students with learning disabilities are allowed to use text-to-speech.
- Modification - instead of using a word processor, the student created a video explaining the content with images, text, and their own voice.
- Redefinition - the student shared their videos with a classroom in another country to teach them about the content and the other classroom could comment back with questions and comments to be answered by the students.

think

At which of these levels do you see students the most engaged? Where is the lesson the most enhanced? At what level did students extend their learning outside of the classroom? As a teacher, what level would you understand without a doubt, the amount of student understanding?

Not every lesson needs to be at the Redefinition level of SAMR, but the higher up the scale your technology integration is, the deeper the student's understanding tends to be.

By combining teaching methods, I can have a better understanding of the level of technology integration and the benefit it can have for student content acquisition.

Reflect for your Eportfolio

I have combined the VARK model, 4 Cs, 3 Es, and the SAMR Model into a set of rubrics that help discern whether a tech tool is a valid resource for its intended purpose.

1. Choose a technology you have used either as a student or a teacher and evaluate it using the Tech Tool Integration Rubrics worksheets based on the current teaching models from this chapter.

A printable and fillable version the Tech Tool Integration Rubrics PDF

are available on my website at

https://www.teachandlearnwithtechnology.com/resources

4 Get Connected - *Teach and Learn with Social Media*

PLN

Dannielle is a first-year teacher. When she graduated from college she was very excited about having her own classroom and teaching all the exciting principles, techniques, and lessons she learned in college. As she enters her 2nd quarter at her new school, she has a fast and furious realization that the teachers around her were teaching unique lessons and she only had a small bag of lessons that every teacher knew and no student was overly excited to do. Are these teachers more creative? Where are they getting these amazing and engaging lesson ideas? Dannielle talked to her teaching partners and they all answered with "The Internet". But WHERE on the Internet?

Anytime I have a question, need an idea or I'm looking for inspiration, I go to my "people". As a teacher, I have found it imperative to create a **PLN or professional learning network**. A PLN utilizes the people around me and the people across the globe as resources to answer questions, give me advice or ideas, inspire me, or collaborate with me to produce something amazing.

Technology has changed our world. Some would say technology has made our world "smaller". With the Internet connecting every corner of the Earth, no teacher should struggle to come up with every lesson on their own or learn about new things alone.

There are many reasons to get connected to others over the Internet:

1. Get lesson ideas and inspiration
2. Share your lesson ideas
3. Get connected to others with the same interests
4. Get connected to others with different experiences/cultures/locations
5. Collaborate with others outside the classroom/city/state/country/ hemisphere…
6. Get answers to questions
7. Keep up on current education and technology trends
8. Grow personally and professionally

Image available at https://www.teachandlearnwithtechnology.com/resources

How to get connected

There are many social media platforms and ways to connect to others online. I am going to suggest just two to get started with. These two platforms are not the only ways to get connected, but they are a great way to begin, for those just getting started with the PLN journey.

Now before you say "I hate social media" or "I don't want my work life mixed with my personal life", I completely understand! That is why I have some basic guidelines listed below, so make sure you finish this chapter before making your accounts.

 Twitter.com

Twitter is a great way to accomplish the 8 reasons listed above, specifically, to find people, companies, or organizations that post content I find valuable. Twitter is both images, videos, and text with less than 280 characters. Unlike Facebook, *most* Twitter profiles are open to viewing by others even if I am not following them. This allows me to see the content of the Twitterer's (people that use Twitter) posts and discern their value compared to my own interests.

1. I encourage you to make a Twitter account by going to https://twitter.com/ or downloading the mobile app.
2. Begin by following me: @jilloutkahill
3. Once you have found me, the next step is to look at the people I follow. Once you follow someone you find of value, chances are,

that person also follows people of like-minded interests. Look at some of these people and again, decide if they can provide value to you in some way and if so, follow them. This is the best way to grow your PLN with other people of similar interests.

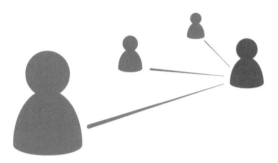

 **Instagram**

Instagram is another social media platform that allows me to connect to others. This platform is dedicated to images and videos with text being an addition to the visual. Instagram's character limit is 150. I can follow people, companies, and organizations on Instagram but the advantage of Instagram is the ability to track hashtags.

A hashtag is a means of tracking a TOPIC versus tracking the people that post about the topic. I can search hashtags on Twitter as well, but I can continue to follow hashtags on Instagram.

1. I encourage you to make an Instagram account (you can use the same username as Twitter)
2. Follow the hashtag **#teachandlearnwithtechnology**

3. There are MANY hashtags to follow on Instagram so once you find a good post, click on the hashtags and decide if that hashtag has content worth following.

At first, I was afraid to post anything and you will probably be the same. This is being a consumer of social media and is a great place to start. You may need to learn the unsaid/unwritten rules of social media before you jump in like you own the place. Watch how others word their posts, use acronyms or abbreviations for long words and use links to other content so they are not plagiarizing. Once I was comfortable with how social media worked, I started re-tweeting or re-sharing a post someone else made. If I added a couple of hashtags it was more likely to be seen by others. Then I made simple text posts followed by an image. Before I knew it, I had lots of people following me and moved from being an exclusive consumer to contributing to the pool. This is when the magic of the PLN happens!

How I use social media for education

I use Twitter for nothing but teaching and professional connections. I follow LOTS of great educators. Feel free to look at the people I follow and you may want to follow them as well. I use Instagram for following professional hashtags. Instagram makes it easy to follow a hashtag whereas Twitter is not as easy. I will only contribute useful, professional, teaching content to these platforms.

What about my personal stuff? I use Facebook and Snapchat for anything personal. This also helps keep my private life PRIVATE.

Social media is the way of the world and there are many ways to manage it, but I HAD to find a way to manage it before it manages me!

Here are some basic guidelines I use for social media:

- Don't mix personal and professional in the same account.

  I made accounts specifically for my personal life and a separate account for my professional life. If you want to maintain anonymity, don't use your name in the username BUT be sure you maintain professionalism in the name you choose. I would suggest initials with some numbers, just your first name with numbers, or just your last name with numbers. This username is the only thing others will have to connect you to your social media so I don't suggest anything too cutesy or possibly misunderstood. You are still a professional person behind your social media persona.

- Don't believe EVERYTHING even if it looks believable.

  I double-check the facts before passing anything on!

- Find a balance between online activity and offline activity.

  A balance means my time online should never be more than my time offline. (This does not include the time I am asleep). This is hard and a constant effort!

- People are not WRONG for disagreeing.

  Everyone is entitled to their opinion. This is what makes the world go around. I am equally entitled to scroll past a post I don't like, agree with, or think is offensive. Just like in the real world, I surround myself with like-minded people.

- Don't argue with people online.

   I scroll past or unfollow people all the time. I interact with LIKE-minded people only.

- Do not be on social media during work or school hours.

   POSTS ARE TIME-STAMPED! People have lost their jobs over this.

- I only post things I am okay with the whole world seeing.

   The world of today AND of the future.

- Never post pictures of students!

   If I must, I am creative with the image such as taking a picture from the back, having them cover their face, or digitally blurring out their faces.

- It's okay to start out as a consumer of content rather than a contributor of content.

We will discuss many more concerns with being online when we cover digital citizenship including student use.

Should I use social media with my students?

Social media platforms have an age limit of 13 due to the Children's Online Privacy Protection Act (COPPA). If my students are under the age of 18, I always get parental permission. I teach my students that it is important they don't lie about their age because many sites are required to protect the data of anyone under the age of 18. This means they don't collect personal data about them or they are not searchable within the platform or on public search engines.

Be a role model on social media

Keep in mind that everything posted on the Internet is there for everyone to see and cannot completely be deleted. Yes, things can be deleted but how many eyes already saw it? Some platforms keep backup files of all data for their own security.

So before pressing that submit button: T.H.I.N.K.

I like to consider how I want people to see me now and in the future. People such as:

- Students
- Students' parents
- Other teachers
- Coaches
- Current and future employers
- Co-workers
- My parents
- My own kids

Image available at https://www.teachandlearnwithtechnology.com/resources

As of January 1, 2022, there were 4.62 billion people on social media and it is growing every day. My colleagues are on social media, my students are on social media and if I want to keep abreast of the latest in any field, this is my quickest, cheapest, and easiest route. As an educator, it will be my responsibility to teach my students responsible use of the Internet and social media, so what better way to do that than to have first-hand experience and be a good role model?

Reflect for your Eportfolio

1. Join Twitter and Instagram with a professional account.
2. Follow @jilloutkahill on Twitter
3. Follow the **#teachandlearnwithtechnology** hashtag on Instagram
4. Make a post on Twitter tagging both me and the hashtag telling me about one thing you would like to gain through social media. It is likely that someone will get you pointed in the right direction. And someday, someone may post a question that you can help with, and the magic continues. ●

You will be asked to share your Twitter and your Instagram handle (username) along with your email address on your eportfolio. Until then, start to build your digital footprint with positive communication with other educators or students pursuing an education degree. This will show evidence of your growth in using social media professionally and give you content to screenshot later if you want.

5 Learning Dictates the Technology - *Teach and Learn with Technology Standards*

Kaitlin is an average 10th-grade student, but because she is the daughter of a military parent, she moves schools every couple of years and sometimes in the middle of a school year. When she goes to a new school there are times when she has already covered similar material and there are times when she feels momentarily lost in the content, but it usually doesn't take her long to get caught up.

think

How is it that Kaitlin can move so often and still keep on track with other 10th graders? It is because most schools have a standards-based curriculum. Originally, 46 states adopted the Common Core State Standards for education. Some states have since abandoned these standards but maintain some kind of state standards-based curriculum that has similarities to the Common Core.

Although content is taught differently depending on teacher or district choice and creativity, Kaitlin can be assessed at the end of the school year on the content presented for that academic year and pass the assessment because she has been taught the material at either one school or the other.

Standards help keep teachers, parents, schools, districts, and states all working together as a team to make sure all students are on track for the next school year. It also helps to collect reliable and comparable data to assure students are progressing.

The Common Core Standards can be found at http://www.corestandards.org/wp-content/uploads/ELA_Standards.pdf .

The states that have adopted the Common Core Standards at some level or another can be found at

https://www.ccrslegislation.info/ccr-state-policy-resources/common-core-status-map/

I make sure I am familiar with my state standards for my respective grade level and/or content area. It is also helpful to read over the standards from the grade level before and after so as to be familiar with where my students are coming from and where they are expected to be the following year.

How do the Common Core Standards pertain to technology?

Technology is integrated into the Common Core Standards rather than being a stand-alone subject. This is important because it goes back to starting with the learning goal first and then choosing a tech tool only if it helps engage, enhance and extend the learning. (Refer to chapter 4) Most technology-integrated standards do not specify WHAT tech tool should be used or how to use it specifically, but rather to use a technology tool to interact, collaborate, research, or present other educational material. In this way, technology does not dictate learning, learning dictates the technology used.

Computer Science Standards

According to Britannica.com: "computer science (is) the study of computers and computing, including their theoretical and algorithmic foundations, hardware and software, and their uses for processing information." (Tucker, et al, 2022) Most states are understanding the integral part technology plays in education and the career world. This has led to the adoption of specific Computer Science Standards. These standards focus on things like the 4 Cs, Internet safety and networks, coding and programming, hardware and software understanding and troubleshooting, data analysis, and laws and ethics specifically pertaining to student technology use.

Unfortunately, at this time very few states mandate preservice teachers to take computer science preparation courses. This means teachers are required to learn right along with the students as they teach the required content.

The adoption of computer science standards and the pandemic of 2020 showed light on the inequity issues of technology in education. Mandating the use and education of technology in public schools means schools will need to purchase and maintain up-to-date technology devices and network capabilities. This can be the largest expense a school has next to salaries. Many states provide funding to schools specifically to teach and assess these standards.

ISTE Standards

The International Society for Technology in Education is a non-profit organization of educators across the world dedicated to promoting the integration of technology into teaching and learning to prepare students for the digital age.

ISTE has developed five sets of standards:

1. ISTE Standards for Students
2. ISTE Standards for Educators
3. ISTE Standards for Education Leaders
4. ISTE Standards for Coaches

5. ISTE Standards for Computational Thinking

Each set of standards are broken down into indicators. These standards arc not grade-specific because they are designed to work with the content areas already being taught in the classroom.

I teach the ISTE standards in my classroom but it is *every* teacher's responsibility to teach the ISTE Standards to all students and to practice the ISTE Standards for Educators.

ISTE has a great website https://www.iste.org/iste-standards full of information so I would highly recommend you spend time on the ISTE website, thinking of ways you are currently practicing these standards and how implementing them can be improved. (ISTE, 2022)

Using Standards

As mentioned earlier, teaching should always start with the goal and not the technology, activity, resources, etc. The goal is the standard. **This is where I start!** What do I want my students to learn?

- When referring to standards be sure to include the numbers of the standard. ie. "CCSS.MATH.CONTENT.2.OA.B.2 Fluently add and subtract within 20 using mental strategies."

Standards can be copied and pasted because it is important that they stay consistent.

- When referring to ISTE standards, specify "ISTE for students, Computational Thinker, Students break problems into component parts".
- Most lessons meet multiple standards. A lesson could meet a Common Core math standard and a Computer Science standard and an ISTE standard all at the same time.

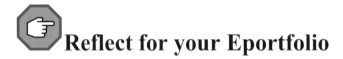 **Reflect for your Eportfolio**

Make a mind map about the ISTE Standards for Educators.

Watch this video for step-by-step directions:

Keep this mind map in your Google Drive. This will be a great addition to your eportfolio.

6 My Classroom is 1:1. Now What? - *Teach and Learning with 1:1 Devices*

Eva was just hired as the new fourth-grade classroom teacher in her hometown. She is excited to finally have her own classroom! She was particularly excited to teach social studies and history. But she was nervous about using technology to teach history. After all, there was no technology back when the explorers roamed the countryside. She knew her school had received a grant and was now 1:1 with iPads and Chromebooks throughout the school. Her administrator expects her and all other teachers in the building to use these devices on a daily basis.

think

Should she use them right away on the first day? How does she keep track of them? How much is she expected to have her students use these devices? Do they take them to specials? Do they take them

©2022 Jill Outka-Hill   Teach and Learn with Technology

home? What happens when something doesn't work right? Or worse, what if a student breaks their device?

These are obviously valid concerns for Eva and many teachers entering the teaching field after 2020. Some schools were already 1:1 before 2020, but after the CARES Act, or the Coronavirus Aid, Relief and Economic Security Act of 2020, many schools opted for using these funds to purchase technology so students were able to continue learning from home if necessary. This was a rapid and drastic change to the way education had previously been done for many schools, teachers, and students.

Remember - Technology is a tool.

As always, keep in mind that technology is a tool to help students learn. Just like paper and pencil are tools used to communicate thoughts and ideas, so is technology. There are times when paper and pencil is still the better tool to use. If technology does nothing more than substitute the use of paper and pencil then why use it? Pencils are much cheaper! I believe the best reason to use technology is to create an opportunity for students to move outside the four walls of the classroom and do something, learn something, or create something that was inconceivable without the use of technology.

My school has been 1:1 since 2016. My fourth-grade students learn about the Oregon Trail every year. Before technology, students would be shown maps, read passages in a textbook and see images in books. This lends itself to a more passive way of learning where students

88

are expected to absorb the information and retain it. Today, with the help of technology, my students can experience the Oregon Trail through virtual reality images and videos that put them into the harsh setting these explorers experienced. They get to hear the sounds of the horses' feet and wagon wheels turning over the hard rocks. They can communicate with museums and experts instantly through video chats giving students the opportunity to hear stories and ask questions. They can use robotics to recreate the trail across the US, video their robot as it travels along the journey, then post the video on the Internet for others to see and ask the students questions about their learning. THIS! This is how technology can transform a classroom from a closed-off space to a world full of opportunity! Which classroom would you rather be in?

If you are fortunate enough to be 1:1, students can stay logged in and should always use the same device. I number each device and check it out to each student so they know they are responsible for it, just like a library book. This also helps both me and my students keep track of each device. We can then use their "tech numbers" for things like lining up or putting things away. I can say "tech numbers 1-5 go get your device".

Teach your expectations before students use technology

Although most students have some kind of experience with screens, I try not to assume all students will know how to use a tablet or computer, just because they are digital natives. Yes, many children today have grown up with a tablet or smartphone in their hands, but oftentimes their experience was purely fun and happened through trial and error. In the classroom, every minute is valuable so every student needs to know how to use their device efficiently and effectively.

Just as a shop teacher wouldn't hand a toolbox full of tools to a student and say "go use these tools", I would not hand technology to a student without giving directions on how to use it safely, understand the purpose of each tool, and what I want them to do with it.

Before students are given access to technology, most schools and/or districts have a standard usage policy that both students and parents must sign before use. This includes access to the Internet and expectations of the appropriate use of a school device. Most will agree that having access to such devices is a privilege and not a right. Be sure to check with your school's technology department or main office before the year begins and before you allow students to use devices. Our school has these forms signed upon registration or renewed at Open House or Back to School nights before students come to school on the first day.

I also make sure students have a clear understanding of why they will be using technology. At home, some of these children use technology to play games, chat with their friends, listen to music, watch videos, and search for anything they happen to think of at the moment. I make sure my students understand that technology in school is used strictly for the purpose of learning about the content covered in class, at that time. All of the activities listed above would be inappropriate during school hours, on a school device.

If students need to look up the dates of the Industrial Revolution while learning about history, this is appropriate. They may even find a video that explains more about this or look at images of inventions from this time period. But the same search is inappropriate during math class.

It is important that students have clear directions of what they should be doing on their devices.

If they are expected to be in an app, they should not be anywhere else but that app. They should have a goal for using the device. What are they looking for? What should they know when they finish? Remember, it is not about using the device, it's about what they can gain from using it.

I have never heard a carpenter say "I used a hammer today". Instead, they would say "I built a house today". Technology is the same. They did not use a computer, they learned about the Industrial Revolution. It's about what my students learned by using the technology.

I use a Safe-Respectful-Responsible Technology Use poster in my classroom and go over each rule before students are allowed to use technology. I also share it with all the teachers in my building. This assures students have the same expectations everywhere they go in the building, whether it is in the classroom, music, library, or anywhere. If this is posted around the building, it also helps substitute teachers to know expectations.

A free copy of this poster can be downloaded on my resource page at
https://www.teachandlearnwithtechnology.com/resources

When a device is misused

think

If a student in shop class misuses the socket wrench, would the teacher take it away and say you can't use it now? Or would they teach the student how to use it correctly because, without it, they won't be able to tighten the necessary bolts?

I believe technology serves a greater purpose than being an avenue of information. If my students in the US are expected to communicate with a classroom in Mexico, they will need the technology to get it done while also learning the value of global communication, an important ISTE standard (see chapter 5). But if a student misused the technology, then it is time to go back and reteach expectations before they use it again. The tool is necessary to communicate with the classroom in Mexico, but parameters may need to be adjusted to make it happen. The length of time the student's technology is removed depends on the misuse, the number of offenses, and the misuse policy of my school. Your school may have a policy in place with warnings, parent contact, and loss of technology. Be sure you know if this policy exists and if not, you may want to initiate one so your school has a consistent policy across the board. Parents with children in different grade levels appreciate the same rules and consequences for all children attending the school.

think

But what if a student is using a tool in a dangerous manner that could hurt him/herself or others? Do you take it away? Consider thinking of it this way- if a student is using a pencil in an unsafe manner that could potentially harm himself/herself or others, would you take it away? Yes! Safety is of utmost importance! But then you reteach safety so they can use it to finish the assignment. This reteaching process with a pencil might look like this:

1. Remove the pencil
2. Replace the pencil with a less sharp tool like a crayon or jumbo pencil.
3. Allow the student to use the pencil under adult supervision only.

4. Allow the student to use the pencil alone with time limits, in a controlled environment.

5. Once the student demonstrates responsible use over time, they can earn the pencil back.

6. Continue to monitor pencil use knowing the potential misuse can occur again.

Now let's consider the misuse of a tablet:

1. Remove the tablet.

2. Replace the tablet with paper and pencil.

3. Allow the student to use the tablet under adult supervision only.

4. Allow the student to use the tablet alone with time limits, in a controlled environment.

5. Once the student demonstrates responsible use over time, they can earn the tablet back.

6. Continue to monitor the tablet use knowing the potential misuse can occur again.

Technology is the same as any other teaching tool.

Using technology loss as a punishment

If a student misuses the technology, it makes sense that the student loses that privilege. If Joey hits Bobby, is late to class, or gets an F on his science test, it does not make sense that confiscating Joey's iPad be an appropriate consequence. The "tool" has nothing to do with the offense. I have seen teachers take technology away because they feel a sense of power or control over their students, but this only confuses the student about their actions and how to resolve them. This goes back to chapter 3 - What is the job of a teacher? **I can never expect to control my students with power.** I can guide my students to make safe, respectful, and responsible decisions so they can be trusted and earn more privileges. **The consequence should match the offense.**

Using technology for free time

Research often talks about "screen time" referring to the amount of time someone is looking at any screen in a given day. However, all screen time is not equal. It can be broken down into 4 categories or PICC:

Passive: watching videos or random scrolling with no particular goal other than passing the time.

Interactive: gaming or researching to learn something

Communication: email, texting, chatting, or video conferencing. Social media can fall under this category if it isn't random scrolling. It should be commenting to others with give-and-take transmission.

Content Creation: making posts, videos, music, art, webpages, coding, or anything for the benefit of others.

I teach my students that each category is different and there are long-term benefits to some more than others.

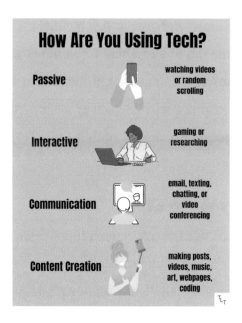

Poster available at https://www.teachandlearnwithtechnology.com/resources

With the rise of technology use in the classroom, I feel it is more important than ever for students to learn to balance their activities with screen and non-screen experiences. **This will not come naturally, so they will need to be taught.** I will have my older students keep track of their screen time and my younger students should be able to identify which category their screen time falls under to determine the value of their time. When a student finishes early or recess is inside, before allowing students to use their device for this time, I have them consider how much time they have been on it that day, and what they plan to do on it and I like to provide an alternative. Oftentimes, technology is an easy crutch to fall upon because it keeps the student busy and quiet but this is when technology becomes a babysitter. **Remember - technology is a tool!**

When choosing to let students be on a device for free time, here are 3 things to consider:

1. **Limit student use to specific apps, websites, or activities**. Having no direction will often lead to misuse. On iPads, I create a folder with problem-solving, creative, and challenging apps. This is a great place for games that relate to classroom content but don't necessarily fit into my lesson plans. For Chromebooks, I create a webpage or use a bookmarking site like Symbaloo.com to hold links to the sites students can visit. I make sure to send them to specific web pages and not just a website, with the understanding they cannot navigate away from the link I gave them. Some sites have some great pages but also have some pages students should not be visiting.

2. **Limit their free time on a device.** Some students finish work much faster than others which could lead to 45 minutes of "free time" where other students barely finish their work. If some students are always finishing early, this is a sign I need to extend their learning. This is when I like to challenge them to learn more, create something to help teach others and understand the content better, or present a problem to solve in regards to the content. I make sure it is fun and rewarding for them but at the same time, they get to use their device and share what they did with others.

3. **Provide other alternatives.** Often times a child (or adult) will turn to their device because it is easy and entertaining. [*Guilty!]*

To combat this, I have seen teachers make sure there are books, board games, building materials, brain teasers, and movement activities in their rooms. Having other alternatives available reinforces the need for balancing screen time with "face time".

Device Management

Ok, you have 25 Chromebooks in your classroom. NOW WHAT? Once I teach my students my expectations, they need a routine. If I establish a routine at the beginning of the year, there is less for me to do during the year.

Consider what you want your class routine to look like. Do you want your students to get their devices when they walk in the door? What do you want them to start working on when they get there? Is there an advantage to arriving early to class and getting work done like sharing their work or helping others? Where do you want them to put the device when it is not in use? Establishing these classroom routines takes the daily questions out of teaching so I can focus on the content.

I make sure students know THEY are responsible for their devices! I cannot be sure all 25 devices are closed out correctly or charged at the end of the day. It is helpful to either have each student plug in their device or have a "Technology Helper" that has that job at the end of the day.

Student: "Mrs. Outka-Hill - my iPad is dead".

Me: "Bummer. What are you going to do?"

Student: "I don't know."

Me: "Well, your class is completing the assignment I sent in Schoology. How are you going to complete your assignment"?

Student: "Can you make me a paper copy?"

Me: "No. I already handed the assignment out to you in Schoology. You didn't charge your device so you can't get to it. How can you complete and turn in your assignment?"

Student: "I guess I can write it on paper."

Me: "Ok. That will work for today. I will put the assignment up on the board but you need to copy both the questions and write down the answers so I know what question you are on."

Student: "Ok." (walking away sulking)

I don't make it convenient for my students to neglect their technology and I always make sure **they are doing more thinking than me!**

My students are busy working on a research project. They have their heads buried in their device and I hear the clicking of little fingers on the keyboards. Suddenly, I remembered something I forgot to tell them earlier. I know if I say it now, only about half will hear me because they are hard at work. This is when I use the phrase "**face-time**". This means I need to see all faces looking at me before I will share, speak, give directions, or whatever it is that I'm doing. This means even little Veronica in the back that is so hard at work, must look up at me before we can all continue. When I'm done talking I say "ok, screen time" notifying them they are free to go back to looking at their screens. This terminology also helps when I'm teaching basic device respect and responsibility. If an adult is addressing them, I tell them it is face-time and disrespectful if they keep their head down.

Another tool I use is a Screen Up and Screen Down sign. Students are often excited to get going on my assignments and will begin before I finish giving all the directions. So I have this on a magnet on the front whiteboard signaling when it is okay to open their device and begin working.

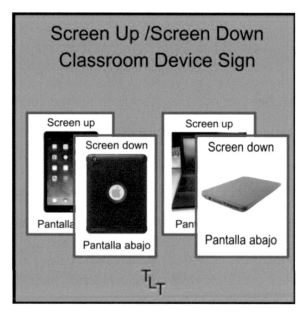

Download this for free at https://www.teachandlearnwithtechnology.com/resources

think

When using technology, how do you keep students from getting off task and going somewhere or doing something they shouldn't be doing? The same way you teach anything else. **You keep them engaged.**

If your students are bored with a pencil and paper what will they do? Find something better to do. If they are bored on the iPad or Chromebook, they will find something better to do.

There are ways to monitor student screens and lock student screens or apps and I will use these to keep tabs on how my students are doing, but you shouldn't need those as a threat to keep students on task. If your students are active in their learning, they won't think of going elsewhere on their devices. It is your responsibility as a teacher to be a step ahead of your students at all times. Have something ready for those that get done early and have a reason to finish for those that lag behind.

As you plan and create lesson plans for your classroom using technology, it is always a good idea to plan for things to go wrong. Have a backup plan if the Internet is out or if a student left their device at home.

When you were in school, do you remember having classes that routinely did the same thing - every - single - day? You could predict the teacher having a worksheet to complete after their lecture or reading before answering questions. My guess is you didn't love these classes as much as the classes that were different each day. Don't be one of these teachers then! Technology gives you the ability to mix it up and do different things every day of the year BUT remember, you don't have to use technology at all - only if it enhances, extends, or engages better than another tool would do. You want students to be excited about coming to your class because you will always have something different for them to do.

☞ Reflect for your Eportfolio

Open a new Google Doc and write out what you would like your students' routine to look like. If you are currently teaching and know what devices are available to you, you can use this in your plan. If you don't know or are not currently in a teaching position, let's assume you will be 1:1. You get to choose the device.

What will your students do with technology when:

1. They walk in the door?
2. You need to talk to them?
3. They need to partner up or be in small groups?
4. They finish the assignment?
5. Their battery dies?
6. They don't have their device?
7. They need to carry their device around the room? (We often think this is more for small children but even older students need directions or they will be dropped)
8. They are not using their device and need to store them away.

If you establish these simple routines at the very beginning of the year, you can spend the rest of your year TEACHING!
Keep this in your Google Drive to add to your eportfolio.

7 We Play the Cards We Are Dealt - *Teach and Learn with No Tech or Low Tech*

My good friend Kim lives just over the border from me in another state. I have been very fortunate to have technology in my classroom for years, but she is not as lucky. Teachers have access to a computer lab and they can check out an iPad and Chromebook mobile lab, but devices are not always available when she wants her students to use them. This has become frustrating at times. So how do we teach technology skills and prepare students for a high-tech world if technology is not always accessible?

One Device Classroom

If the teacher's device is the only technology available, this can still be a valuable asset to your students. This device can be used in small groups or centers.

The first thing I would do is create user accounts for teachers, substitute teachers, and students using this device. Whether the computer is a MAC or PC, the teacher should always have a password-protected account to keep private information and settings from being changed by click-happy people. (kids and adults)

Jobs

Before students use the computer, make sure your expectations are clear for what they should be getting done, how they should do it, the amount of time they will have, and who is responsible for each part. It is important to assign each student a job. Here are some example jobs:

- Driver and navigator (2)
- Typer, clicker, and reader (3)
- Researcher, reporter, recorder, and director (4)
  Or any variation of these. Each student needs to have a specific job so no one is sitting idle and no one dominates or takes over the assignment.

These jobs should rotate so students are not always doing the same job for all projects.

Time Limit

Students should have a set amount of time to allow all students access to the device. This is when I use timers on my teacher's computer and put them up on the projector. I have a sample timer on my resource page. https://www.teachandlearnwithtechnology.com/resources

Collaborate

Access to a single computer is ideal for using a shared Google Doc. Each group can contribute something valuable but something different that all students can benefit from. By using a Google Doc, you can go into the History and see what each group did.

Create

If the classroom has access to a single tablet, this is a great opportunity for students to be creative and produce audio or video products to showcase their knowledge. Allow them to come up with how they want to demonstrate their learning to the class. You will be amazed at some of the ideas they come up with!

 **Tech Tools**

Plickers is a great, free, assessment tool for classrooms that have a single device with a camera. It allows a teacher to run a clicker-like scenario to quickly assess understanding. Each student holds a piece of

paper with Plicker codes printed on them and the teacher can scan the classroom with the camera, reading the codes each student holds up. It reads them quickly and then gives a summary of answers on the Plickers screen. This is an affordable and fun way for students to answer multiple-choice questions and the teacher can get immediate feedback from their responses.

Low-Tech Classroom

A low-tech classroom is one with a limited number of devices for all students to share. A common scenario is a classroom having 3 or 4 computers sitting in the back of the room. Unfortunately, these devices are often outdated and possibly mismatched with a variety of software loaded. This can be much like the one-device classroom but you can have groups running simultaneously.

Logins

This is a good time to discuss student logins. More and more apps, programs, and testing sites are tracking student progress. This means they will each have individual usernames and passwords for each platform they use. This can be a management nightmare if not approached strategically.

My district assigns usernames and passwords to all elementary-level students. Once a student leaves elementary school, they can choose their own passwords but the usernames are still assigned to eliminate confusion. Students are not allowed to visit websites or apps and create their own accounts. Many education platforms have a teacher dashboard that allows them to see the results of their work, track their usage, and manage their logins.

Non-readers will need help logging into most platforms. Fortunately, many companies are aware of this and are starting to create QR codes (we will discuss these later in Chapter 9) for students to scan and get right into their accounts. Those that haven't gotten on board with this yet will require an adult to help them log in. This can be done at a small center with a teacher, teacher aide, or older student helper.

If students are 1:1, they can log in to apps and sites and stay logged in. If they are in secondary, they should be using a lock screen to prevent others from getting into their device.

When students are sharing devices in a low-tech classroom, it is important for students to not only understand how to log in but also how to log OUT! It's a frustrating day to find out Joey did all his work on Jane's account. Following routines helps eliminate this. Login - do your work - log out. I like to tell students it's like closing the door to their house. You would never leave the front door wide open for people to come in and out without you knowing. This is what staying logged in is like! Log out so no one can walk into your house/account.

Logins should never be posted for everyone else to see. Teach students to remember their logins or keep them in a safe place such as a journal or a notes app. This is a life skill that will only get more complicated so start now! After all, how many logins do you have?

BTW - be a good example for your students and never leave your logins on a sticky note on your computer screen. If this isn't you, I know you've seen this! I'm sure YOUR students are angels and would never be mischievous, but students have been known to use these logins to adjust test scores or worse.

No Tech Classroom

Students can still learn the 4 C's (from Chapter 3) without technology. Teaching technology concepts without the use of technology is called an "unplugged lesson". Code.org is a great website with many resources and ideas about how to teach unplugged lessons. Code.org offers a FREE workshop to teachers by going to https://code.org/professional-development-workshops.

This workshop focuses on elementary teachers but the concepts can be modified and used elsewhere.

Here are some things to keep in mind whether you have one device or a low-tech classroom:

Do:
- Focus on group, project-based learning

- Ask for donations of old devices
- Project/present student work
- Get a wireless keyboard and mouse
- Create stations
- Use cameras, audio players and old keyboards as additional stations
- Have students prepare materials away from the computer/device
- Use task cards to give directions
- Allow students to be "experts" and teach other
- Create pairs or small groups with specific roles:
  - keyboard
  - mouse
  - director
  - screen reader
  - editor

Don't:

- Let it collect dust
- Use it only as a teacher machine
- Use it as a reward or for free time
- Use it only for games

In the Classroom

My youngest students color a Blank Keyboard worksheet with the letters of their name in a different color. My older students color the same worksheet according to home row fingers.

I also print a Giant Keyboard for my students to put together like a puzzle on the floor.

These keyboards are available at
https://www.teachandlearnwithtechnology.com/resources

My favorite unplugged lesson was using a simple deck of cards. This is how I introduced coding and algorithms each year. If I held up a red card, students would clap and if I held up a black card, students would jump up. Obviously, each action can be changed but this is a good chance to get your students up out of their chairs! Once students had this down (10 cards or so) then I would change the actions to hearts = clap over your head, diamonds = clap the floor, spades = jump to the right, and clubs = jump to the left. The older the students were, the faster I would show the cards. Then I would show two cards together and they had to read left to right and do that card first. I later acquired multiple decks of cards and put students in small groups. This way they could choose their own actions. I had students doing pushups, dancing the floss, and making animal sounds. As simple as this sounds, it is a great opportunity for students to be creative, communicate, collaborate, and think critically.

Teacher tip: carry a deck of cards with you for when students are transitioning in the hallway or waiting in line. An idle mind can be a dangerous thing so keep those minds busy and having fun with the activity. They won't realize they are learning too! ●

Teachers like Kim and other teachers in similar situations with little or no technology in their classroom will need to be more creative to teach students computer science skills, but it can absolutely be done. We don't always have the luxury of having the latest and greatest in our classrooms. We play the cards we are dealt and continue to do the very best we can for our students.

Reflect for your Eportfolio

1. Go to https://code.org/curriculum/unplugged

2. Browse the numerous unplugged lessons. Find one that matches your grade level and if you are a current teacher, try it in your classroom!

3. Open a Google Doc and explain the difference between:

- 1:1 Classrooms
- Low tech classrooms
- No tech classrooms

4. Give specific details about how you would handle each scenario.

Keep this handy for your eportfolio.

8 We Don't Want to Learn, We Just Want to Play - *Teach and Learn with Gamification*

My third graders came meandering into my classroom. It was a cold day outside and they had been doing test prep in their classrooms so you could see the despair in both the students' and teacher's eyes. They were tired and needed a break. Chris comes in with his shoulders looking slouched more than normal. "Mrs. Outka-Hill, we have had a long day and we're tired. We don't want to learn, we just want to play that game on the computer today."

When the school bell rings at the end of the day, some students head to the locker rooms to get ready for sports, a few have miscellaneous lessons or activities, and the rest head home or to their respective places. Guess what many of these students are doing after school? Yep, they are on their phones or tablets and either communicating or GAMING.

Gamification is using the elements of games in an educational environment. Gaming tends to receive a bad rap from those that don't understand it. Although I am a proponent of monitoring screen time and getting physical activity, I do see many benefits of gaming:

- Games bring to life a world of competition, problem-solving, improvement, and multitasking. Now, don't get me wrong, not all games are created equal! But the idea of students working toward a goal is not necessarily a bad thing. These students (and oh yes adults like their games too) will spend hours trying something one way, failing, trying it another way, failing again, and continuing to try until they are successful. Doesn't this follow the "try, try again" philosophy we often tell young people and encourages a growth mindset? They are using strategy to accomplish a task while often communicating with other players, whether as team members or against them as challengers. They earn points for things well done and lose points for mistakes made. All of these things keep people coming back, again and again, to be better than before.

- Let's face it - games are fun! When developed correctly, students don't realize they are learning. When graphics, audio, characters, and a good storyline are all combined with a challenge mixed in with some educational content, classtimes fly by!

- A game will keep a score based on student success. This means a student with a high score is obviously demonstrating an understanding of the content whereas a student with a lower score may be struggling. Games can be a replacement for a worksheet or quiz. The score reflects understanding. I'm not saying all tests should be gamified, but most students would enjoy playing a game over doing a worksheet any day.

- Another benefit is that gamification provides differentiation for students. This means those students that know their math facts can whizz through the first couple of levels to get to the harder questions that are more appropriate for their level, while those struggling learners can stay at the beginning levels to practice what they need.

- Games provide immediate feedback to the students as they play. When a student completes a worksheet it could be days or even weeks before they know how they did. They learn that they either understand the content or they don't. How many go back and revisit what they did to learn from their mistakes? Not many. But in a game situation, students can only go on if they answer correctly. That means they know immediately whether they understand the content or if they need to change something. This gives the teacher an opportunity to reteach the student so they learn it, can continue on, and reap the rewards of practicing it correctly rather than risk the chance of practicing an entire page incorrectly, only to find out the following week they were doing it wrong all along.

What does it take to make a "good" game?

Whether a game is played on a board, on a court, or on a computer, there are some basic characteristics that keep people coming back. They should be:

- **Independently challenging.** This means that either the person or the team must use strategy to play better, or sometimes worse, than the other players. There should be multiple ways to achieve the goal. If everyone ended with the exact same results it wouldn't be a challenge.

- **Competitive**. Many games are played against other players but sometimes the competition is about improvement over time. This is a competition against yourself!

- **Rewards.** This is usually done with points but can also be done by earning more resources, and badges, or opening up new options or levels.

- **Progressive**. All games should start easy. This helps teach the rules at a slow pace but gradually gets harder as the game goes on. If students get stuck, there should be some way for students to acquire pieces of knowledge to help them be successful.

- **Have an end goal.** Sometimes winning with the most points at the end of the time limit is the end goal but sometimes it's about completing a task, progressing to a new level, or earning something at each level.

- **Appealing**. Whether it is visually esthetic with graphics and colors or the audio is exciting with sound effects and music or the combinations of the two, long gone are the days of the black and green screen of the Oregon Trail Game. Oh the days of DOS!

- **Have a storyline or theme.** This isn't always necessary but works well in a school setting. Your game can be based on a novel the class is reading or a popular movie. This helps when it comes to team names, levels, and rewards. It also helps to keep students interested because they have a sense of attachment.

- **A cross between realism and fantasy.** Kids love to use their imaginations. A game setting is a great way to encourage creativity while still teaching the principles of real-world communication and collaboration. This also helps to keep it FUN!

Non-digital gamification

Michelle had a class of fourth graders that seemed to struggle to get along. They were a diverse class with varying interests, economics, and academics. They seemed to argue about the smallest things because they each saw the world differently - until Michelle gamified her classroom. She made four teams out of her class of 20. Each team was chosen randomly and they were given a team name. Team names could be based on books, movies, themes, or classroom content. The teacher chose these names to eliminate the possibility of arguing from the very beginning and were based on the book she was reading to them. Each team was allowed to arrange their desks however they wanted but together as a team. Then Michelle shared how each team could earn points. These were not just following regular classroom expectations, because all students are expected to do these, but rather it was going above and beyond.

- If a student was helpful to another student or staff member, their team got a point.
- If a student got a compliment from an adult, the team got a point.
- If every team member kept their desk clean, they got a point.
- If the team was caught using appropriate conflict resolutions, they got a point.
- If all team members turned their assignment in on time, they got a point.
- On Friday, each team could "cash in" their points for a fun Friday activity or treat.

At first, Michelle only had means of gaining points. This allowed teams to get acquainted with the "game". Then teams started losing points for being disrespectful, unsafe, or irresponsible. She told them it was the responsibility of the team to help each teammate make good choices for the better of the team. Within three weeks, her diverse class had cohesion and was no longer thinking of just themselves. Of course, issues would arise, but she would meet with the whole team and they would discuss what was best for everyone on the team. Eventually, students that started out the year being rude and selfish to others were now encouraging and Michelle was sure to notice when these students did something - ANYTHING positive to reward the team with a point. As the year progressed, she changed the criteria and value of points to keep the game interesting. Because just like any game, it must get harder to maintain interest. She would switch up the teams a couple of times a year and ask the students if they had additional ideas on how to make points and ideas for rewards on Friday. Her students suggested doing jobs for the school, such as taking out the trash for other classrooms, taking lunch trays to the kitchen, or helping younger students put on their coats and backpacks at the end of the day. They chose to have a movie day if all groups earned a minimum number of points. Her game grew into something she never imagined it would! **She and her students were having fun and they were cohesive beyond her expectations.**

Tom was a sixth-grade teacher that created a similar atmosphere in his room, but rather than points, he taught his students the value of money. His game was based on class economics. Each item was worth a dollar amount and students had to earn their rent for the week. If students didn't pay their rent, they lost their desks and worked on the floor. Those that earned extra money could purchase a bouncy ball in place of a regular chair, a window seat for their desk, or access to the coveted colored gel pens. He always added new items to be purchased and more responsibility to pay for. He introduced taxes, expenses, savings, and even investments. He had a student that wanted to loan another student money so was able to introduce the concept of interest. **What an amazing learning opportunity for these students!**

There are many ways to use gamification in your classroom. Some of the best games are the ones students come up with on their own. You are only limited to your ability to be flexible and creative.

Digital Gamification

Digital games are not only educational, fun, and challenging but are extremely engaging. Games can be played on computers, tablets, or smartphones. There are TONS of websites and apps that teach educational content with more coming out daily. When choosing which games are best for your classroom, you can always start with the 3 Es X2 from Chapter 3.

If you were to look up "math games" online, you would never be able to sift through all the results. So, I like to look up specific content, read reviews, listen to what other teachers are using, and have success with, and of course, I refer to my PLN.

I don't recommend putting too many game apps on a tablet at one time. I like to switch them out occasionally to keep students interested. Also, consider you may have some students that don't like games. The excitement may be uncomfortable and cause anxiety. I like to use **the 80/20 rule**:

- 80% of your apps should be productivity apps. These are apps that are NOT content-specific. They help the student do something or demonstrate their learning in any class and use it multiple times with different results.

- 20% of your apps should be game apps. These apps are content-specific and once the student has played the game, they know it and the results will always be similar. Students get bored with these apps once they are played.

Infographic available at https://www.teachandlearnwithtechnology.com/resources

When considering the price of an app, there can be in-app purchases or subscriptions, so be sure to budget for these. I like the free apps, but the trade-off is there will be advertisements. Someone has to pay for the development of that app.

Be sure to read reviews. You can save yourself a whole lot of time if you know an app crashes or you only get two levels for free before having to pay for it.

Gamification

- Encourages problem-solving
- Allows for differentiation
- Provides immediate feedback to students
- Is a FUN way to learn!

The game Chris wanted to play when he came into my room was a math game. It covered progressively harder math facts where characters travel through 3D tunnels, collected gems, and defeated the monsters, all while answering multiplication questions before the time runs out. Once they get to the end of the tunnel, they get a chest of gold coins that can be used to purchase more tools to defeat the upcoming monsters at the next level. Knowing just this, does this game:

- Make a good game?
- Serve as a form of assessment?
- Teach a content area or standard?
- Teach soft skills?
- Encourage creativity?

So Chris didn't realize he was learning when he played this game. It was just fun to him. Would you rather play this game or complete a worksheet with questions in nice, long rows?

 **Tech Tools**

Here is a Symbaloo of a very small sample of gamification websites. <u>Symbaloo.com</u> is a FREE website that lets you make links to websites and arrange them visually. This is a good alternative for teachers that want to send links to their students without creating a full website. It can also be a place to store bookmarks for either teacher or student. By sharing a link to a Symbaloo page, someone can access many other pages.

My favorite games, both digital and unplugged, are escape rooms. Escape rooms are done in small groups with a time limit to complete a series of tasks before they reach the end of the challenge. I have created multiple escape rooms about a variety of content ranging from digital citizenship to specific Common Core Standards. Although the amount of time and effort put into creating an escape room can be extensive, the reward is amazing! My students always leave understanding the content and are able to practice the 4 Cs. There are many pre-made escape rooms online but with the use of Google Apps, you can create your own. My students love escape rooms and even I had my sixth graders create one based on a famous scientist.

☞ Reflect for your Eportfolio

1. Go to my Symbaloo page: <u>EDU Games</u>

2. Play a game. Complete a level, or a task, or play to the end so you have a score or something that says you completed the game.

3. Share your thoughts about gamification with me! Make a post on Twitter tagging both me @jilloutkahill and the hashtag **<u>#teachandlearnwithtechnology</u>** telling me:

   a. What game you played (a link to the webpage is great and if you can tag the company, you may get a reply from them).

   b. What standard or content your game covered.

   c. What students would learn from playing this game.

Take a screenshot of your post AND of the game you played to include in your eportfolio.

9 How Teachers Clone Themselves - *Teach and Learn with Audio and Video Technology*

Audio

Rafael was teaching his class about the use of proper nouns. He gave a few examples and then the class was invited to share some of their own examples. The students seemed to understand and they went on to complete the lesson when the door to the classroom opened and Katie came in. She had just arrived at school from a dentist appointment. In the past, Rafael would have Katie read the chapter in the book that covers this material or he would need to teach her 1:1 while the class went on or waited. Fortunately, Rafael recorded the lecture. While he got the rest of the class going on their assignment, Katie listened to what she missed and was right up to speed with the rest of the class. Rafael also keeps these recordings for students to revisit later if they forget or are confused, and these recordings are great for students to review before an assessment. By recording himself, Rafael has cloned himself, in a sense, to teach without having to be physically present.

In Chapter 3 we discussed the VARK model. The traditional classroom tends to focus on the read/write learners whereas the modern classroom is focusing on all learning types. Some students prefer to hear the teacher talk about a topic and explain things in a way they can connect to. These students tend to connect through conversation and can benefit from a classroom lecture environment. Recording yourself removes the strain of being in multiple places for multiple students at the same time.

Audio is also a great way for these students to demonstrate their understanding. Audio students would rather record themselves giving examples of the content being taught than write it down. You can often discover which students are audio learners by hearing them whisper the directions out loud or you see them wait for the teacher to explain the directions. These students are often the ones that write something down and go back to read it aloud to themselves. Why not allow these students to record their answer so they can replay them, hear how it sounds, and turn them in? Obviously, this is a great alternative for visually impaired students and students for whom English is a new language. (covered more in Chapter 12)

This leads me to another advantage of audio. We have identified communication as one of the 4 Cs from Chapter 3. Communication is vital for success in everything personal and professional. Allowing students to record their voices, gives them an opportunity to develop that voice.

Listen here for a sample audio file - <u>Audio in the Classroom</u>

Also available at <u>https://www.teachandlearnwithtechnology.com/resources</u>

Rafael has a typical class of varying personalities. He has Jade, who loves to have all the right answers and is obviously an audio person because she sometimes struggles with NOT using her voice during class. Then there is Karter, who is a quiet student who has learned to let Jade have all the answers because then he doesn't have to speak in front of the class. It's not that he doesn't know the answer, he just hasn't developed the confidence to share it out loud yet. When Rafael finishes giving directions, he tells his students to go to their desks or a comfortable corner on the floor and record themselves using three plural nouns. Their sentences must be about a trip they have taken. This makes each student do their own work, and have a close connection to the content, and students love talking about things personal to them. If they make a mistake they can go back and do it again without the pressure of others hearing. He tells them to listen to their recording, make sure they speak clearly and with intonation and turn in the one sentence they did the best. Students can turn their audio files in using Google Drive, a shared file, or on an LMS, all covered in Chapter 2. Karter and Jade both have the same opportunity to develop their speaking skills and show competence in proper nouns. Rafael enjoys listening to students and the things that interest them most. He later uses these in conversations to make connections and build relationships with his students.

So how does Rafael get his audio files to his students?

Tech Tools

Audio Memos App

For mobile device users, this app is free, comes on most Apple mobile devices, and can be downloaded to an Android as well. After downloading the app, open it up and press the red Record button. When you finish, the button turns to a Stop button. Each audio file is saved separately, can be renamed, and is date and time-stamped. Then to download the audio file, tap on the file you want to share > press the three dots > and tap Share. You can email, text, and send it to other apps like your Google Drive or Airdrop it to another device, which is my favorite in the "Apple World". These files are .m4a files. This does cause some trouble with inserting into Google Slides or other platforms that prefer .mp3 files. There are many free web-based file converters. I like to use Online-Convert.com. Just upload the .m4a to the website, scroll to the bottom and click START. You don't need to change any settings to do a simple file conversion.

 **Online Voice Recorder**

For desktop users, this is a free web-based tool. Open the website https://online-voice-recorder.com/ and press the red Record button. You may need to allow the use of your microphone the first time. Your audio will begin recording and you have the ability to either pause your recording or stop it and listen to it. If you like the recording, choose Save, if not, you can click the X in the right corner. This file downloads as a .mp3 file so there is no need to convert it.

These audio files can be uploaded to an LMS, a shared folder in Google Drive, a website, or directly with the students. But what if you want to use this audio file with the youngest of learners that don't have Google Drives and don't share files?

 **QR Codes**

Quick response codes or QR codes are barcodes that represent information. This information isn't just for audio files. It can be text, website URLs, social media links, contact details, or a number of other things.

Most smartphones and tablets with a camera will scan a QR code by just POINTING the camera app at the code. No need to take a picture! Just put the code in the camera's view and a window or text should pop up letting you click on the link. If you are using a Kindle you will need to download a free QR code scanner from the Play Store. If your camera is not scanning the QR codes, try closing the app out and trying again. If it still doesn't scan you may need to turn it on in the settings. On an Apple device go to Settings > Camera > Scan QR Codes. On an Android go to Settings > System Apps > Camera > Scan QR Codes. The Chrome browser is also a scanner or you can download a free scanner app, but be aware of ads if young students are using the app.

You have seen these QR codes throughout this book for easy and fast access to digital files. There are infinite ways of using QR codes in your classroom.

I used QR codes for a quick link to my "Out of the Room" form. I wanted to know what students left my room, at what time, and for what reason, but I didn't want to manage this while I was teaching. My students knew only one person could be out at a time so they could scan my code, complete the form and leave. All I asked is that they showed me a quick hand signal before they left. This gave me an opportunity to teach some basic American Sign Language like "toilet", "nurse" and "office".

I also used QR codes for reading books aloud to young students. A teacher can record themself reading the book, make a QR code, and tape it to the back of the book. Now students can have their teacher read to them anytime. This is also great for sending books home with students that don't have someone to read to them.

I placed QR codes on posters or worksheets to read words or directions out loud. I can also send students to a YouTube video that reviews a concept or explains something in more detail.

QR codes are great for keeping information hidden from students until they are ready to see it. I would create a QR code to an answer key so students could check their work once it was complete. I know what you're thinking - they could cheat using that! I suppose they could, but they had to show how they got there and if they didn't know the content during classwork, it would be obvious at test time. This gave students an opportunity to work through their mistakes.

Scavenger hunts are super fun for both teachers and students. I used them at the beginning of the year to learn about my room. I would place QR codes around the room and if students followed the scavenger hunt correctly, each QR code would give them a letter and then would spell out a word.

Of course, QR codes are a quick and easy way to send students to a specific website. I would make the QR code and then put it up on my interactive board for everyone to see. This way students could scan it from where they were sitting.

There are many ways to incorporate QR codes into your classroom to quickly send students any information.

Rafael used audio files in his classroom to keep students current that missed class, share his voice in multiple places, allow his students to find and practice using their voice, and turn in audio files for assignments. This makes grading assignments fun for Rafael too. He can hear his students' voices and even reply to them with his voice if he chooses. The options are endless, encourage the 4 Cs, and meet the 3 Es X2. Definitely a win-win for Rafael and his students.

✊ Reflect for your Eportfolio

Here is how Rafael created and shared his audio files:

1. He recorded his voice using the Online Voice Recorder and placed each file in a shared Google folder.

2. Then he went to each audio file and copied the shared URL of that file. This can be done by opening the file in Drive > clicking the 3 dots in the top right > Share > change the access to Anyone with the link (is a viewer). Then click Copy Link.

3. He used a free website, such as https://www.qr-code-generator.com/ to create his codes. Once he pastes the URL into the page, the QR code was created. He then clicked download and he had a .jpg file he could use almost anywhere.

Now it's your turn. Practice making an audio file and turning it into a QR code for your classroom.

Make an audio file using either of the two resources listed here. Your audio file should be about using audio in your classroom and why it is important. Be sure to put this in your own words and how it would specifically relate to your grade level and content area. Save your audio file to your Google Drive, and create a QR code from the shared URL.

Keep both your audio file and QR code in your Google Drive to add to your eportfolio.

Video

No matter what the grade level of my students, I almost always started the class off with a video. I usually kept them short, 2-5 minutes, but this helped transition my students from whatever they were doing in the classroom, hallway, or playground. Video provided an opportunity to focus my students on the topic for that day. My youngest students would often watch a music video that would teach them something with a catchy, rhyming tune. "Here we go, oh, oh - seasons of the year." Yep - that one will be stuck in my head for a while now! My older students would watch a video about how to do something in my classroom such as circuitry or coding or the history behind technology or about an inventor.

Some of the best videos were the ones I made myself. Although intimidating at first, it seemed my students enjoyed watching me on screen. I would play the video on my interactive board before I would say much at all. This way they could "guess" what we were doing that day, share what they knew and ask questions. This turned their focus to our topic and we were off and running.

Here is a fun example of a video I created using Flip for my first graders. They were learning about how technology changes over time. If you use the trends on video streaming sites like YouTube, you are more likely to grab your students' attention. This is a box opening video:

A link to this video is also available on
https://www.teachandlearnwithtechnology.com/resources

We know many students are visual learners. These students like to see pictures, organize according to color, and pay closer attention to the slides during a classroom lecture than what the teacher is saying. Textbooks have tried to accommodate these learners by including photos and graphs to display information. Although it is better than no visuals, it really doesn't meet the 3 Es X2. This is where the world of video comes in!

Ask any student about videos and they will likely mention YouTube. YouTube.com is the second largest search engine behind Google with 100 hours of video being uploaded every minute! (Global Reach, 2020) We live in an amazing time where there are people that know things that want to share what they know with others FOR FREE. Watching YouTube today is like watching TV in the '80s and '90s. Yes, I'm dating myself here but the fact that people like to experience entertainment with video has been a long-time hobby for many. What used to be Saturday morning cartoons has now turned into anytime and anything someone wants.

This also means there is some great educational content out there on YouTube-land. But what if your district has YouTube blocked?

Unfortunately, there is some not-so-good content on YouTube as well, which has led some schools and districts to block the platform entirely. Personally, I see this as a tragedy due to also blocking the valuable content, but this is one of the only ways districts can regulate what is seen on campus. However, this doesn't prevent students from going to YouTube off campus and they need to be taught how to use the site. This will be covered more in Chapter 13.

There are many other video sites that contain good educational content:

Big Think

Brightstorm

CosmoLearning

FunBrain

Howcast

Internet Archive

Khan Academy

MathTV

NeoK12

PBS

Storyline Online

TeacherTube

TED

WatchKnowLearn

Wonder How To

…and many, many more!

When you send students to YouTube, you run the risk of them viewing content that was not intended for them to view. There are recommended videos listed on the side that can be either distracting or inappropriate for young students. The comment section can have inappropriate words, advertisements can lead students astray and the video that plays after yours, may not be what you want them to see.

This should be a digital citizenship conversation with all grade levels. Make sure your expectations of staying on that video are clear and your students have a specific task to do while using this tool.

There are **clean viewing** sites designed to block suggested videos, comments, and advertisements from YouTube videos. These free sites remove everything except the video and title making the focus stay where you intended. I call these clean viewing sites because it cleans up all the extra unnecessary "stuff".

Here are three clean viewing sites I use:

https://watchkin.com

https://safeshare.tv/

http://viewpure.com/

Let's compare one of my YouTube videos played directly from YouTube and one I have placed into a clean viewing site.
Here is a screenshot of the very end of one of my videos on my YouTube channel:

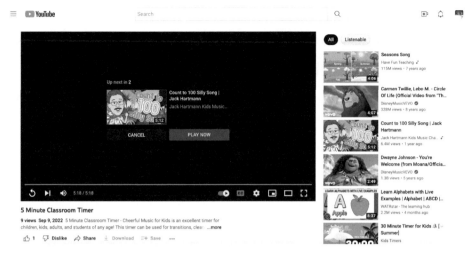

Notice the video that plays immediately after mine and the enticing recommended videos on the right. These are not what I want students to watch. Students would also be able to scroll through any comments left below the video.

I copied the URL from the YouTube page and pasted it into Watchkin. Here is the exact same video opened up from Watchkin:

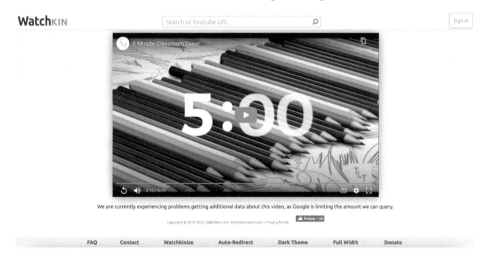

No video plays when mine ends, no recommended videos, and no likes, comments, etc. Just the video you want your students to watch.

And YES, you can make a QR code from it! There is a unique URL created from Watchkin for each video. You can copy that URL and create a QR code for it. But what if YouTube is blocked? Does this still work? Unfortunately no, it needs to connect back to YouTube for the original video.

Copyright Material

Since we are covering audio and video in this chapter, let's consider a couple of common scenarios:

1. It's the week before Christmas/winter break and teachers are frantically finishing report cards while students are more restless than ever.
2. You have to be gone for a couple days and would rather not create sub plans since no one can teach it quite like you.
3. Your students have been working really hard and they earned a class reward.

A common solution to these is often "I'll just show a movie". But before you break into your home collection of children's animated movies, or login to your personal streaming service, you need to know there are copyright laws that protect not just videos but all creative works.

Laws are in place to protect the rights of creators. Educators are not above these laws and districts have paid fines due to breaking these laws. Teachers can lose their jobs and their teaching license if caught in violation. This does not mean you can't show any movies in your classroom, it simply means you need to do your own research on the particular video you are showing and the means in which you are showing it.

- You should always check with your district to find out if they have policies in place for showing movies in your classroom.
- The movies you play should have educational value and relate to the content your students are covering.
- Personal streaming accounts are designed for individual use. Some schools have education accounts to stream content to many users.
- There are education streaming and video options available to assure there are no advertisements and all content is school appropriate.
- Keep in mind that the rules for face-to-face instruction with videos are different from showing videos to students remotely.
- When in doubt - ASK FIRST. Sometimes we are tempted to ask for forgiveness rather than permission, but this is one case that forgiveness may not be an option. Check with your IT department and your library media specialist before showing any movies or videos in question.

I am not providing legal advice within this book, but I am providing a heads-up to things you may not otherwise consider. I highly recommend you do your own due diligence when using copyright protected media in your class.

☞ Reflect for your Eportfolio

1. Find a video on YouTube that relates to your grade level and

content area. Copy the URL and put it into a clean viewing site.

2. Open a Google Doc and write a short paragraph about why using video in your classroom is important and some of the things to consider.

3. Copy and paste the URL to your clean viewing video into your document and explain why using these sites are beneficial.

You will add this document to your eportfolio.

 Tech Tools

If you can't find the video you want or your district blocks your video sites, then it's time to pick up a camera and make one for yourself. Your students love seeing YOU on screen! It doesn't have to have professional lighting or microphones. Just use your smartphone, tablet, or computer camera in a well-lit place. Natural light is best. If the recess bell goes off in the background - no worries, keep going! You are still getting your message across.

You can also use **screencast** software to record your screen. Screencasting creates a video from the actions that occur on your screen.

- iPhones and iPads come with a screen recording tool in your Control Center. If you don't see it you may need to add it to your Control Center in your Settings. The microphone is off by default so if you want it to record your voice, hold your finger down over the button, then tap Microphone Off to turn it red and activate the microphone.

- If you want to screen record from a computer, I like using **Quicktime Player.** This program is free and comes with most Apple computers, but can also be downloaded to a Windows device. Open the program, click File on the top menu bar > New Screen Recording. You can choose to record your entire screen, just a specific window or a section of your screen. Make sure your microphone is selected under Options.

- Screencastify is a Chrome extension that can be used on Chromebooks. Although you are limited to the number and length of your videos, I like that it can also use your front-facing camera to put a thumbnail of you in the bottom corner. This helps make it more personal.

- Loom is another site that has a free plan with limited videos and length but I like the editing tools that come with it.

- Flipgrid is now called Flip and although this isn't made for screencasting, it works GREAT! You can add text, record from your camera, record your screen and post it to a collaborative, safe, space for students to practice making videos and using good digital citizenship in a controlled environment. My students have had SO MUCH fun with this site! It provides a good alternative to having students record their voice or audio and then share it.

Using audio and video in your classroom is a great way to prepare students for their future which we know is becoming more video oriented. Using audio and video in the classroom meets the 3 Es X2 and saves the teacher time by being in more than one place at a time. When teachers allow students to use audio and video, it meets their VARK learning style and encourages the 4 Cs. Not to mention it is SUPER FUN!

10 Expand the Walls of Your Classroom - *Teach and Learn with AR/VR and Virtual Field Trips*

We know using and learning about audio and video help students prepare for skills needed in their future. Now let's turn it up a notch and add a dimension. 3-dimensional video is often referred to as augmented reality (AR) or virtual reality (VR).

Virtual Field Trips

think

If you could take your students anywhere in the world to explore places, see people, learn things, and experience cultures outside the classroom, where would you go? I know what you're saying: "I can't take 25 students traveling to remote places of the world!" How about if you didn't have to leave the classroom? And it was FREE?

Some students might not ever have the opportunity to see the world but you can bring the world to them with virtual field trips. **Virtual field trips** are a way to explore the universe through the world wide web, from any location, and using any Internet-connected device through video and audio.

There are three types of virtual field trips:

1. Pre-packaged - These virtual field trips:

- have specific and consistent content
- are often directed by the creator
- are available at any time
- will assure any number of students will get basically the same content, even at different times.

Mallory was teaching ecosystems to her 2nd-grade class. She teaches in the midwest, where many of her students have never been to the ocean. She found a 360-degree YouTube video of a scuba diver swimming through a coral reef rich with plant and animal life. The students watched as the diver left his boat, swam through the reef, and pointed to specific animals and plants before resurfacing. The end of the video was an interview with the diver naming some of the fish and the history of the area. Each student watched the video and was able to identify two living and two non-living things essential to this ecosystem.

2. Un-packaged - These virtual field trips:

- do not have specific content and sometimes have no content at all
- are self-paced and self-directed
- are available anytime
- will likely result in students getting different results at different times

 Tech Tools

Mallory decided to take her students on another virtual field trip using **Google Earth**. This app has an enormous collection of satellite and street-view images. She had her students visit a volcanic island called Ambrym in the Archipelago of Vanuatu. The explorers within the video took 360-degree images while they explored and even descended into the crater. Her students were able to look around at different parts of the volcano including a lava lake, a walk along the crater edge, and they learned about a nearby volcanic beach and village. Each student viewed the images on their own and was able to identify something unique that others may not have seen. When they finished, they went to the live webcam of Kīlauea Hawaii.

3. Real Time - These virtual field trips:

- Are based on what the presenter says and shares

- Can be interactive with the students but still presenter driven
- Availability is dependent upon the presenter
- Are generally as a full class

To complete Mallory's ecosystem unit, she contacted a university near her and spoke to a professor in the ecology department. He was more than happy to hop on a virtual call and answer questions her students had about ecosystems in their area.

Virtual field trips have become more popular since the rise in technology during the COVID pandemic. We have all learned that connecting with people across the world is simple and free. There is no reason to keep our students confined to the four walls of our classrooms, even if we can't afford to take them places.

Augmented Reality

Augmented reality augments or changes our reality to enhance it or add something. **Virtual reality** completely removes our reality and places us into another virtual space.

Clyde is teaching anatomy and physiology to his middle school students. The curriculum provides textbooks, posters, videos, and even plastic replicas of the human body. These work okay, but the students struggle to see how the amazing human body works together. Clyde found a couple of augmented reality tools to allow his students to explore further.

Tech Tools

Clyde purchased some **Merge Cubes** and brought them into his classroom. These foam cubes contain images and lines that serve as codes on each side of the cube that interact with an app. When the camera on the device is pointed at the cube through the app, it gives the illusion that the cube turns into something else. The cubes are very versatile in the content it displays and you can even create your own content with an add-on. Clyde's students would open the **Merge Explorer app** and point the camera at the foam block and suddenly it appeared as though they were holding a live and beating heart. You could see the arteries and veins moving blood through the heart as the valves opened and closed with each beat. They then opened another game on the app that allowed them to see where the heart sits in relation to the lungs and how deoxygenated blood is pumped to the lungs and oxygenated blood is pumped from the lungs to travel out to the body. They turned the cube around looking at each side of the heart and lungs understanding the complexity of each intricate part.

The cubes are fairly inexpensive and some apps are free whereas some cost a couple of dollars each. Don't have a Merge Cube? No problem. You can download and print a paper version from their website here:

https://support.mergeedu.com/hc/en-us/articles/360052933492-Making-a
-Merge-Paper-Cube

      Ready to make your own content using Merge Cube? CoSpaces
Edu is where teachers and students can make their own content,
classrooms can be managed through the platform and the possibilities are
endless!

      What about augmented reality for younger students?
The Merge Cube has great value for young students too. They can turn
the merge cube into a moving and interactive solar system or an
aquarium with fish swimming around the coral in emerald blue water.

But what other AR apps are used for young learners?

 **Chatterpix** is a free app that turns ANYTHING into a talking object.

My preschool students were learning about pumpkins. They had learned pumpkins come from seeds planted in the ground and are not just orange but can be many different colors. They learned you can make pumpkin pie and pumpkin soup and of course, they can carve a jack-o-lantern. To make this assessment fun for the students and teachers, we brought in a pumpkin, set it on the table, and had the students open the Chatterpix app. They started by taking a picture of the pumpkin. Then they drew where they wanted the mouth to be and pressed the record button. They had 30 seconds to tell me everything they knew about pumpkins. When they finished they got to choose some eyes or some glasses to put on the pumpkin and they tapped the play button. Suddenly their pumpkin looked like it was talking and sounded just like them! They could tap the download button and it becomes a video to share with me through an LMS, shared folder, or airdrop.

I have had students take a picture of their writing, of shapes in the room, their projects, and creations, or even pieces of equipment on the playground to review school rules.

Chatterpix is a fun and easy way to assess student understanding!

QuiverVision.com has many free and premium paper coloring pages of all different content that students can color. Then they open the Quiver app, point the camera at their page and their image comes to life! Students can see the alligator they colored for A and the bear for B exactly how they colored it, moving around their screen and making sounds. Students can learn letters, numbers, life cycles, the layers of the Earth, the parts of a cell, or even how a DC motor works.

The **Narrator AR** app encourages the youngest of learners to write and then turns their writing into animation. Just print out the paper and start writing! Students will see either a rocket or a unicorn move around their screen and then re-write their name, letters, numbers, pictures they drew, or any number of things. Their website has FREE and paid lesson plans that are print and follow-ready.

What if you want to make your own content? The options are endless for how you can turn simple lessons into something that literally jumps off the page! With a bit more time and tech-savvy-ness, you can combine photos and videos with QR codes and animation to make something truly amazing for your students!

Sites such as BlippAR.com, MyWebAR.com, and Assemblr.com are just a few of the many augmented reality creation tools that allow you to turn everyday items into an interactive world on screen. Create your own or find creative content others have already made. Most sites have FREE and paid plans, an app to download and read the trigger object or image, and a drag-and-drop interface so you can have an AR project ready for your students to not just see but literally experience. What better way to bring the world to your students and prepare them with the tools for their future.

Virtual Reality

Now let's talk about virtual reality. This is where the students are placed into a completely different environment (or so it seems) through the use of technology.

Virtual reality often uses a headset to close out the existing environment and replace it with real or fictional virtual images and sounds. Some headsets are very expensive and still in the development phases. Virtual reality is a growing and evolving industry and may someday change the way education looks. VR has the potential to immerse students into a realistic and interactive world like no other that provides learning opportunities hardly fathomable.

Although these forms of VR are quite expensive at this time, Google has developed a cardboard version that wraps around a smartphone. This device is more affordable for a classroom but is limited in its capabilities - for now. At the time of writing this, Google has a site: https://arvr.google.com/ that tells of headset options and apps to go with it.

But you don't need a headset to experience virtual reality. Although not totally immersive, with a mobile device such as an iPad, students can experience what it would be like to draw a 3-dimensional shape in space, then rotate the shape on its axis while measuring the length of each side with a virtual ruler. They can feel like a real astronaut while walking across the surface of the moon, experience the mammoth-sized elephant of Africa as it walks within inches of you, or swim with the sharks in the dark depths of the ocean - all while sitting in your classroom.

With the use of augmented and virtual reality, students can interact and immerse themselves into the content of the world, all while staying in your classroom.

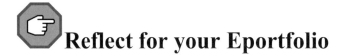 **Reflect for your Eportfolio**

1. Download the Chatterpix app to your smartphone or tablet and find something you can make "talk".
2. Use the short 30 seconds to teach shapes, letters, numbers, character traits or other ELA concepts, book summaries, policies

and procedures, art/music/PE concepts, history, math, and social studies. The list is endless! If you don't have an object near you, you can find an image online and take a picture, then teach with the talking object.

3. Download the video and save it to your Google Drive.

You will add this video to your eportfolio.

11 Real-World Lessons - *Teach and Learn with STEM, Computational Thinking, and Coding*

think

Before we move forward, I want you to think about the word "technology". What comes to mind? Computers? Mobile phones? Wires and electricity? Robots? Rooms full of blinking lights and metal?

Although this is what most people think, you are only partially right.

According to Dictionary.com the first recorded use of the word "technology" was in Greece in 1605-15. I'm pretty sure they weren't texting it to their friends. So what does the word really mean? Merriam-Webster defines it as:

a: the practical application of knowledge especially in a particular area: ENGINEERING sense 2 medical technology

b: a capability given by the practical application of knowledge. A car's fuel-saving technology

2 a manner of accomplishing a task, especially using technical processes, methods, or knowledge. New technologies for information storage

3: the specialized aspects of a particular field of endeavor. Educational technology (Merriam-Webster., n.d.)

When I explain technology to young students, I tell them "technology is a tool that solves a problem or makes something easier".

think

So let's consider the following 3 images. Do they solve a problem or make something better?

Does it seem the most important parts of the definition of technology may be the words "application" and "engineering"? This is AGAIN where it is so important to reiterate the importance of:

Technology is not about tools…   **…it's about what students are learning, doing, creating, solving, planning and THINKING!**

It's also important to remember what a teacher's job is (from Chapter 3).

STEM

Amy is a third-grade teacher that knows the importance of each content area, but like so many teachers, she struggles with fitting all that content into the day. Between specials, recess, lunch, special events, holidays, and assemblies, she has to find time to teach, assess and reteach: math, reading, writing, science, and social studies. There just isn't enough time in the day!

One day her students were on the playground and complained to her about a corner of the basketball court eroding away. Rather than dismiss her students or send them to the building custodian, she used this as an opportunity to talk about erosion, which was on her list of topics for the week. She asked them why they thought it was happening and if they had possible solutions. The conversation continued into the classroom where they talked about how water erodes different types of materials and how gravity has caused the water run-off from the building to pass by the basketball court, washing away the dirt from underneath. They returned to the playground later that day with a measuring tape to measure the affected area and how far the water should be diverted in a different direction. She then had her students research possible solutions online before coming up with ideas to solve the problem. Their writing assignment was to write a letter to the principal and building custodian about possible solutions. Amy learned the value of STEM. This is combining content areas into a single lesson, specifically science, technology, engineering, and mathematics. **Very rarely is content separated in the real world.** Amy combined erosion from science, researching online from technology, playground design from engineering, and measuring from math. AND her students could relate to a real-world problem that was meaningful to them. To truly be "STEM" it must combine 2 or more standards from the subject areas and the more, the better.

There are a number of acronyms that depict the combination of content areas:

STEM = Science Technology Engineering & Mathematics

STEAM = Science Technology Engineering Art & Mathematics

STREAM = Science Technology Reading Engineering Art & Mathematics

STREAMR = Science Technology Reading Engineering Art Mathematics & Recreation

- STEM lessons are interdisciplinary, real-world issues that students resolve using the **engineering design process or EDP**.
1. **Ask** what the problem is and if there are any constraints
2. **Imagine** possible solutions, brainstorm ideas, and choose the best one

3. **Plan** your solution with diagrams and collecting materials
4. **Create** your solution by following the plan and testing it
5. **Improve** your solution by deciding what can work better

Then ask again, what is the current problem based on our solution? And the cycle continues.

Image available at https://www.teachandlearnwithtechnology.com/resources

- Failure is a natural part of STEM lessons, but rather than focus on the failure, students focus on what they learned and continue through the EDP.
- STEM lessons often have more than one solution.

- Students will generally be hands-on with STEM lessons. There is a lot of DOING and not just learning about how others did it.
- STEM lessons can be a whole classroom, group, or partner activity
- The 4 Cs are at the core of STEM

Amy's classroom was more engaged than she had seen in a long time. There was so much noise and excitement! At the end of the day, her students were still talking about their plans and couldn't wait to hear back from their principal. A teacher from across the hall came over to see what the excitement was about and Amy learned her husband was an engineer. He came to visit Amy's classroom the next week to teach students about his job as an engineer. The corner of the playground was soon fixed with a suggestion from the class and her students not only understood their content standards but had pride in knowing they helped fix their playground.

STEM lessons can go on and on due to the nature of the EDP. This is when I would often tell my students "we are never finished with our learning, but we have to be done for the day".

STEM is not designed to be a stand-alone class but rather a great opportunity for teacher collaboration to make it really benefit students. A STEM/technology teacher/facilitator is responsible for knowing and teaching the technology tools and knowing how to fix them when something goes wrong. Classroom teachers are responsible for the content standards and enforcing proper vocabulary usage.

Computational Thinking

Computational Thinking is a real-world application to problem-solving. Amy's classroom solved a real-world problem, but there is a process of being able to think through the problem and the solution to get a result.

According to ISTE (International Society for Technology in Education), Computational Thinking or CT is:

- Formulating problems in a way that enables us to use a computer and other tools to help solve them
- Logically organizing and analyzing data
- Representing data through abstractions such as models and simulations
- Automating solutions through algorithmic thinking (a series of ordered steps)
- Identifying, analyzing, and implementing possible solutions with the goal of achieving the most efficient and effective combination of steps and resources
- Generalizing and transferring this problem-solving process to a wide variety of problems (ISTE, 2022)

By identifying the problem, breaking it up into small pieces and giving specific directions to each step, students can use computational thinking to solve all kinds of problems.

We can search far and wide for real-world problems to solve, and although these are connected to our student's world, there is another option that students LOVE even more! Remember talking about gamification in Chapter 8?

Some students in Amy's class could think through the process of the playground getting fixed and the order in which things needed to be done, but she noticed some students could not comprehend how some steps were needed first, such as clearing out the currently loose material before repouring new asphalt. To allow her students to practice problem-solving and computational thinking, she introduced coding to her classroom.

Coding

Computational thinking does not always require the use of coding but it can be a great way for students to visualize the problem-solving that occurs during the process in a more concrete way.

Coding or computer programming is writing a set of instructions that a computer understands so it will perform a task. But each instruction needs to be in the correct order and set to the correct parameters to function properly.

As we prepare our students for a world of technology, coding is an integral part of this learning process. Most real-world coding is text-based with numbers, letters, and symbols that look like a foreign language to most of us.

For example, a website's code may look like this:

```
▼<div class="QZ3zWd">
  ▼<div class="fktJzd AKpWA yMcSQd Ly6Unf G9Qloe XeSM4 XxIgdb f0U46b"
    jsname="UzWXSb" data-uses-custom-theme="false" data-legacy-theme-name=
    "QualityBasics" data-legacy-theme-font-kit="Light" data-legacy-theme-
    color-kit="Custom" jscontroller="Md9ENb" jsaction="gsiSmd:Ffcznf;yj5fU
    d:cpPetb;HNXL3:q0Vyke;e2SXKd:IPDu5e;BdXpgd:nhk7K;rcuQ6b:WYd;"> flex
    ▶<header id="atIdViewHeader">…</header>
    ▼<div role="main" tabindex="-1" class="UtePc RCETm" dir="ltr" aria-
      hidden="false">
      ▼<section id="h.5b9700d4f269773d_18" class="yaqOZd LB7kq cJgDec nyKB
        yd 013XJf" style>
        ▶<div class="Nu95r">…</div>
        ▶<div class="mYVXT">…</div>
        </section>
      ▶<section id="h.5b9700d4f269773d_25" class="yaqOZd lQAHbd" style>…
        </section>
      ▶<section id="h.5b9700d4f269773d_41" class="yaqOZd cJgDec nyKByd"
        style>…</section>
      ▶<section id="h.1476f36c3639ed6a_0" class="yaqOZd qeLZfd" style>…
        </section>
      ▶<section id="h.5b9700d4f269773d_45" class="yaqOZd" style>…
```

Coding can still be taught to young students with block-based codes. A block of code can represent each of the codes above to look like this:

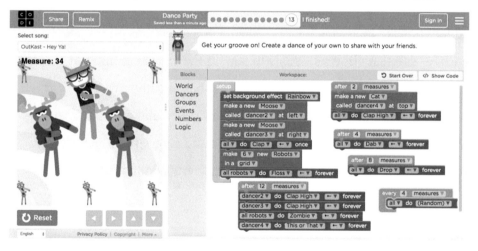

Students drag and drop blocks that represent text codes and they use them in the same sequence as text codes essentially having the same result. There are many apps and websites that allow students to practice drag-and-drop coding or block coding. The code is provided, you just have to put it in the right order. This is a great progression to learning code.

 **Tech Tools**

The previous image was taken from a website called Code.org. This site is dedicated to teaching students computer science through coding. The games begin with having a character move one space, then turn, then do an action and each skill is a block of code that is added to make their character do a sequence of actions on screen. This is a FREE site that allows students to start at the very beginning of block-based coding and progress into text-based coding like Java programming and even into artificial intelligence and machine learning. Code.org progresses through many levels and a variety of games. But what if you want your students to code their own animations?

My 6th-grade students were reading a book for their ELA teacher. It was the fifth book that year and they had done all the traditional book reports and projects based on previously read books. So we decided to recreate our favorite scene from the book using Scratch.mit.edu. Students drew their settings, characters, and props. They coded their characters, using block codes, to move around the screen and say quotes from the book. Each project needed to include a conflict from the book and how the conflict was resolved. My students enjoyed sharing their creativity and although each was very different from the others, we all knew exactly what part of the book each student recreated. My students were so proud of their work, we invited parents to come in and see their "book reports". The parents were amazed by the animation and coding that went into this project! I had a number of parents say they had no idea their child was able to do this and acknowledged how they were going to be so much more prepared for their future with these skills.

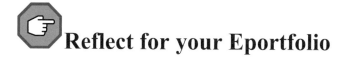Reflect for your Eportfolio

1. Go to https://studio.code.org/s/coursea-2022

2. Complete the coding lessons starting at #2 Learn to Drag and Drop (notice the unplugged lessons if you have no/low tech in your classroom). Get as far as you can in 20 minutes. Don't forget to look at the SHOW CODE on the congratulations screen to see what code you would have written in text-based code.

3. When you finish, take a screenshot and put this in your Google Drive.

4. Then write a paragraph about teaching STEM, computational thinking, and why coding is essential to preparing students for their future.

12 A Lifeline to Education - *Teach Special Needs Students with Technology*

Assistive Technology

Differentiated instruction is the process of meeting individual students' needs by tailoring the instruction to meet them where they are in order to make them successful in their learning. It is a tailored education for all. We know that no two students are alike and it is our responsibility to make sure every student is successful. This means we may need to provide extra help for some, additional resources for others and some students may need a completely different approach. Due to specific circumstances, some students may need assistive technology tools in order to learn. **Assistive technology** is any tool that is used to improve someone's capabilities, usually due to a disability.

Image available at https://www.teachandlearnwithtechnology.com/resources

According to the US Department of Education, the **Individuals with Disabilities Education Act (IDEA)** is a law or statute that "makes available a free appropriate public education to eligible children with disabilities throughout the nation and ensures special education and related services to those children. " (IDEA, n.d.)

When a student has special needs, educators, parents, and professionals will draw up an **Individualized Education Plan (IEP)** outlining the needs of that student and how the school can make them

more successful. As an educator, you can expect to participate in the development and follow-through of IEPs for a number of your students. These plans must be followed according to law and serve to protect the rights of all students. Assistive technology is often an integral part of an IEP to accommodate students with special needs. This is a valuable tool for students with both physical or learning disabilities.

Keep in mind the word "technology" actually means "tool", so some of these devices are high-tech and some can be low-tech. Technology has impacted the lives of many people with disabilities, allowing them to move, communicate and function successfully in school and society.

There are many apps in the App Store specifically for special education ranging from free to $299+. Sometimes things as simple as changing the size of the font or the teacher wearing a microphone when they speak can meet the needs of students. Many assistive technology tools are built into computers and mobile devices as Accessibility Options. They can also be added or available online.

 **Tech Tools**

Text to Speech software reads aloud digital text. Although many of us are quick to think of the visually impaired, this is a great tool for emerging or slow readers, or for students with dyslexia, auditory learners, or those students that English is not their primary language.

- Mac - Voiceover

  This is a setting within the System preferences of the computer under Accessibility

- PC - Voice Narrator

Turn this on by going to Settings > Ease of Access > Narrator

- Chromebook - ChromeVox

    Press Control + Alt + z to turn on the screen reader from any page

- Speechify app

    This is only one of the thousands of text to speech apps available

    on tablets

Each tool comes with a variety of options for the voice, speed, and dialect of the reader.

Side-note: As a busy person, I use text-to-speech capability to read articles or webpages aloud while I multitask. This has become an invaluable tool for me both personally and professionally.

Speech to Text software turns audio speech to text. Again, it is natural to think of how this can benefit the hearing impaired but it can also be helpful for visual learners, students with physical disabilities in their arms or hands that struggle with fine-motor skills, or students that find expressing themselves with writing as a challenge.

- Mac - Voice Dictation

    This is a setting within the System preferences of the computer

    under Keyboard

- PC - Speech Recognition

    Start > Settings > Time & language >

    Speech

- Chromebook - Enable Dictation

    Settings > Advanced > Accessibility

- Keyboard microphone on mobile devices

- Dictation app

This is one of many speech-to-text apps available in app stores

- https://dictation.io/speech is a free website that allows you to type or paste text that will be read aloud

- Closed captioning

This is the text that appears on the screen from either television or from an online video. I use this nearly every time I play a YouTube video for my students. This helps reach those read/write students that may benefit from watching a video and reading the text on the screen. This  can be turned on by the CC at the bottom of the video screen.

Word Prediction is a feature most devices have but we would be most familiar with it in texting. It is what shows up as suggestions when we type something into a mobile device. There tends to be a recurring pattern to common language and our devices attempt to foresee the next word we might want to use. Most of us see this as a convenience to short-hand typing, but those that struggle with language and coming up with the necessary words to communicate effectively can use this tool to get their thoughts out in the text that is also grammatically correct.

Spell check is what we commonly refer to as auto-correct. Although it can be comical or sometimes annoying, it can also be a valuable tool for those that struggle with spelling. I will confess, this is not my strong suit! I like to consider myself a savvy communicator but I will still use the spell check features on documents, emails, and almost anything text written just because there is no reason to have misspellings with the technology available to us today!

Audio Recorders was covered in depth in Chapter 9. It is important for audio learners to have a way to hear their teachers speak, whether sitting at their desks or at home working on assignments. Having the voice of the teacher there to walk them through a process, using the appropriate vocabulary, tone and familiar patterns can often mean the difference between a student understanding or giving up. For visually impaired students, this could be their lifeline to education! The two tools listed below are covered in depth in Chapter 9.

- Audio Memos app
- Online Voice Recorder

Timers not only help teachers stay on schedule but they can help students with transitions. Time is an abstract concept that many students wrestle with.

Paul was a student that did well in my class but struggled to transition out of my class and back to the classroom. He would often yell, get angry and even get physical because this was a stressful time for him. I like to think it was because "time flies when you're having fun" so he didn't think he got his full allotted time when he came to see me. By setting a timer on his iPad, he could watch the minutes tick down, understand he had a full class, and he would know it was time to clean up when the timer got to 0. I saw such a difference in how this student responded that I began setting a timer for 5 minutes at the end of EVERY class so students like him knew how much time they had to clean up. If I noticed Paul was deep into his work, I would occasionally give him some verbal cues to bring his awareness to the time so it didn't come as a shock. Timers can be used for just about anything to keep students focused and give a visual representation of when something will come to an end.

- https://www.online-stopwatch.com/ is a website I will project up on my interactive board that has a visual hourglass to represent the time along with the numbers.
- There are a number of clock app timer apps but most tablets come with a built-in clock that also functions as a timer.
- I created my own 5-minute YouTube video with no advertisements. You can access it on my resource page at https://www.teachandlearnwithtechnology.com/resources

Sound Systems benefit students with hearing aids or any hearing disability because when a teacher speaks into a microphone and has all audio projected into the room via speakers, they can hear it clearly regardless of where the teacher stands or the direction they are facing. Not only do these students benefit but ALL students will benefit. When teachers use a microphone, they no longer have to yell to project their voices. Yes, your throat will thank you at the end of the day, but your students will also start seeing you as a calm and approachable person.

I once had a high school teacher that I thought was an unhappy person because she yelled all the time. As the semester went on, I had the opportunity to get to know her better in a small group setting and she was so friendly. One day a student asked her why she yelled at them so much and I remember her looking confused and then saying she wasn't yelling, she just wanted to make sure everyone heard her.

Microphone/headphones/hearing aids (all device compatible) can be separated from sound systems because there are some microphones that connect directly to hearing aids. The technology of hearing devices has improved dramatically over the years so now students can adjust their device from a mobile app and they are so small. Some are even surgically implanted so you would never know they have them. This is why it is so important to make sure you read and know every one of your student's IEPs.

There are many, many more technological advances in assistive technology. This is only a list of the tools I would use on a daily basis in my classroom. I encourage you to explore these tools on your own and use them in your classroom, not only for the students with identified disabilities but also to help those students that struggle in areas that by the use of a simple technology tool can either make or break their success.

Technology and English Language Learners

English language learners (ELL) are students that speak a language other than English as their first language. These students may speak one other language (bilingual) or many other languages (multilingual) but they are learning how to speak English.

You may have students that speak English at school and another language at home. This means these students only get to practice using their English at school, but they can still adequately communicate with other students and teachers. These students may need a little extra support such as repeating things slower or repeating in a simpler way. These students may make grammatical mistakes when speaking and writing but just need more instruction and practice.

You may have students just coming to the United States and speak no English at all. These students are called **newcomers**. These students, regardless of age, will first be concerned with basic survival skills and not necessarily the multiplication skills you are covering in math right now. They need to tell you they are cold, hungry, or need to use the restroom. The language barrier for these students can often result in behavior issues or low self-esteem.

Technology can help both the student and teacher have a more productive class day, make the student feel comfortable, and be successful. Many of these tools are things we have already discussed, such as audio, closed captioned, spell check, etc. However, there are also tools specific to language learners.

Students learning a new language can build off the knowledge of their primary language. This means that even though they speak another language, there are still pronouns, verbs, and adjectives that make up the structure of a sentence. Obviously, these words are pronounced and spelled differently but a dog is still a dog. Knowing this, communicating with students and allowing them time to learn language fundamentals is made easier with technology. With immediate feedback, real-world application, and lots of support from those around them, these students can be successful in learning English.

 **Tech Tools**

Duolingo App and Website

There are a number of apps and websites that allow people to practice a new language but I like the way Duolingo lets you practice with multiple choice, text, audio recordings, and listening practice and it is free. It tracks your progress and moves along at a progressive pace to introduce new words at the appropriate time and includes many of the features we discussed in Chapter 8 about gamification. Duolingo has incorporated many of these features to keep you coming back to learn more. Many people have learned a new language with this tool.

Google Translator App and Website

Jose was a newcomer to my classroom and although I knew some simple Spanish, I was far from a fluent speaker. My biggest struggle was understanding him when he would talk fast and his words would run together. I loaded the Google Translator app on his iPad and mine. For the first couple of weeks we would try to understand each other and if not, go to the app to help us communicate.

I have a two-part disclaimer here:

1. Translation apps are not always accurate! But they were helpful in getting the main idea across to someone who would otherwise not have understood.

2. Translator apps should not become a crutch for either the student or the teacher.

Jose's classroom teacher was fluent in Spanish and spoke to him in his native language frequently. By doing this, Jose was not learning the English language and began having behavior issues. He didn't get along with his peers and would often act out in class. Once his teacher started speaking to him slowly and progressively in English, Jose began learning the language. His classmates would help him learn words for basic functioning in school, he began to make friends, and his behaviors improved.

Teaching ELLs is another topic in itself and will not be covered in depth here, but understanding that a student must use the language to learn it is vital. This is where teaching mindset and the ability to fail are so important. The entire classroom must be supportive and before long, these students will fit right into the amazing dynamic of your classroom.

Reflect for your Eportfolio

1. Go back to the previous paragraph. Consider the ways you could use technology to deliver this paragraph to hearing or visually impaired students or to an ELL student. Try one of the methods I suggested in this chapter.

2. Open a Google Doc and write a paragraph about ways you could use technology to accommodate students needing assistive technology and for ELLs in your classroom.

3. List a couple of examples and explain why it's important to meet these students where they are in their learning process.

4. Save this in your Google Drive to put into your eportfolio.

13 Be Prepared for the Digital World - *Teach and Learn Digital Citizenship*

- What year did Abraham Lincoln become president?
- What is the structure of a carbon atom?
- Who invented the printing press?

These are all legitimate questions that may come up in a classroom setting or at home when students are working on assignments. Gone are the days students would walk down the hall to the library to research these topics in hopes of finding an answer. They have a small, flat rectangular object in their pockets that they can either verbally ask or type in and have an answer in less time than it would take to get permission to go to that library. Now don't get me wrong - libraries and books absolutely have their place and their value, but when a student is in need of a quick fact, this is not their go-to source of information. Today they instinctively reach for their gadget. Since 1998, the word "Google" has been used as a verb and was officially added to the Oxford English Dictionary, according to Wired.com. (Heffernan, 2017) This means every student born after 1998 has been "Googling" their entire life! This has come with both advantages and disadvantages. I have already talked about many of the advantages in other chapters, so this chapter will be dedicated to the disadvantages and the actions we can take to lessen the impact these have on our society.

Conner was a fifth-grade student and quite tech-savvy. We were working on a word processing assignment based on a fictional Halloween story they wrote in class before coming to the computer lab to type and format it. He wanted an image to go along with his narrative so he quickly did a Google image search. Without missing a beat, I saw his tablet swiftly turn upside down and he covered it with his arms on the table. His face was a stark shade of red and his eyes looked at me intently as though he didn't know what to say. I calmly walked to his desk and asked if everything was okay.

"I just saw something on my iPad that I don't think I should be seeing," he answered back in a half-whisper.

"Ok, thanks for telling me, let me take a look", I calmly replied as I picked up his iPad. The image he was referring to, although was not the worst I'd seen from a spontaneous Google search but was offensive to him nonetheless.

"I can see how this image doesn't make you feel comfortable, let's try adding some keywords to your search to narrow down the images you get". I scrolled past the image and we talked about adding words such as "for kids" or "clipart" and he was able to find a more appropriate image for his story.

Conner behaved EXACTLY how I had taught all my students to handle this situation. In Chapter 6, we talked about establishing classroom expectations with technology. This is when I teach every student, in grades pre-k and up, how to be a good digital citizen. Each grade level gets a little more intensive and gradually builds on the previous year. By the time my students are searching the web on their own, they know they are browsing a world mostly intended for adults by adults. Although there is great content intended for kids, they will need to be careful getting there and staying there. I compare this with the toy aisle at the store. They all know how to get there and they know the aisles to stay in before they get into the automotive section. My students know that if they go down the wrong aisle at the store, they leave that aisle right away and get back to where the merchandise is for kids. If something happens that makes them feel uncomfortable, they need to tell an adult right away. This is the same with doing web searches.

- If they go to a site that isn't intended for kids, they need to leave right away.
- If they feel uncomfortable about something, they need to tell an adult.

Most importantly, I tell my students they are never in trouble for unintentionally going to the wrong website or getting an inappropriate photo in their image search.

However, they are responsible for:

- Not staying there (click back or close it out)

- Not telling or sharing it with friends
- Telling an adult immediately.

This way, a student can't get in trouble later for something they accidentally saw on their device. I also tell them these rules should apply at home. Most students have a phone or device they access the Internet from at home and while many parents are actively involved in what their child does online, there are many that are not.

My students know I have 3 classroom rules and they apply to both being present in my classroom and being present online.

- Be safe
- Be respectful
- Be responsible

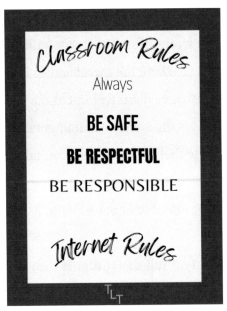

Image available at https://www.teachandlearnwithtechnology.com/resources

I have never found a behavior that didn't fall under one of these 3 rules and oftentimes they fall under more than one.

While many schools and districts do all they can to prevent inappropriate content from entering our schools, this content won't be filtered out when the child is at home. I teach them it is important to listen to that feeling they get in their gut when they know something isn't right. This is their body telling them to do something different and if they are on the Internet, I give them the actions: Get out, don't share with friends, and tell an adult.

When it comes to my very youngest students, I stick to the shopping analogy. I ask them if they have ever been shopping. Of course, all of them raise their hand so they can all relate. I asked them if they knew *everyone* in the store. Living in a rural area, it is not uncommon to see familiar faces in public places but inevitably, there will be strangers present. Most students have heard of "stranger danger" and know not to talk to people they don't know, so this is a great place to review this. I then ask them how many have been on the Internet. Most raise their hand and some are not quite sure what that means. I remind them of the mouse practice games they recently played in my class. "Oh yes," they all remembered.

I told them that the game was on the Internet. So I asked, "What would you do if a stranger started talking to you in the store?"

"We would not talk to them and tell our parents". They answered.

"Great, now if you don't know everyone in a small town grocery store, then there is no way you would know everyone in a store as big as the WORLD. Because the Internet is all over the world, and everyone is a part of it. The Internet is like a store the size of the world. If a stranger sends you a message on the Internet, you do the exact same thing as you would in a store. You don't talk to them and you tell an adult right away".

The size of the Internet is way beyond a child's and even an adult's comprehension, but knowing it is bigger than our local grocery store puts things into terms my students can somewhat relate to.

 **Tech Tools**

The scope and sequence of teaching digital citizenship could be an entire book in itself, so I am not going to get into this here. However, I will recommend the site I go to for advice and resources.

The **commonsensemedia.org** website "is the leading independent nonprofit organization dedicated to helping kids thrive in a world of media and technology. We empower parents, teachers, and policymakers by providing unbiased information, trusted advice, and innovative tools to help them harness the power of media and technology as a positive force in all kids' lives." (Common Sense Media, n.d)

I absolutely love this site! Not just because it has a complete scope and sequence with ready-made lessons and assessments for free, but because they are topics my students can relate to and enjoy doing. They separate content into grade bands and each builds on the previous.

We live in a digital world and as all of us connect and communicate online, we make up a thriving community of digital users. This makes each and every one of us digital citizens of this ever-expanding digital community. As a classroom teacher, it is your responsibility to teach digital citizenship to your students, even if you have a technology teacher or media specialist. If every teacher that uses technology in their room teaches digital citizenship at the beginning of the year, our students would be better prepared for the digital world they will forever reside within.

☞ Reflect for your Eportfolio

1. Go to

   https://www.commonsense.org/education/scope-and-sequence

2. Choose the Grade Band you are interested in teaching. Choose one of the lesson plans provided and deep dive into the lesson. You will find videos, handouts, teacher resources, and everything you need to teach the lesson and it is completely FREE.

3. Open a Google Doc and write about what digital citizenship will look like in your classroom and explain how you would teach the Common Sense Media lesson you chose. (Don't copy the lesson in your explanation, just refer to it).

14 Is That Legal? - *Teach and Learn Student Federal Privacy Laws*

think

Let's think of a couple of hypothetical scenarios:

Scenario #1: You are a classroom teacher (of any grade level). At the end of the day, a sibling of one of your students walks in the door. "I'm Joey's brother and he was out sick today so I'm supposed to come by and pick up his test score. He's been wondering how he scored and I told him I'd grab it for him". Is it okay for you to release Joey's test score to his older brother?

Scenario #2: Your fourth-grade students are studying US history and you want them to create a timeline. You found a great free app they can use online. Can your students use this app to make their projects?

Scenario #3: Schools understand children will be accessing the Internet at home, which is more than likely an unfiltered environment. However, your school has content filters on their internet that prevents students from accessing images and content that could be deemed "inappropriate". In doing this, the filters will occasionally filter out good, educational content. Is this suitable for the school to do?

When it comes to following federal laws in a school, it is not the sole responsibility of administrators, but it also falls on the teachers that tend to work more with the students, parents, and daily happenings in the classroom. In order to answer the above scenarios, we need to dive into 3 very important federal laws that help keep our students safe.

FERPA

FERPA stands for Family Educational Rights and Privacy Act. This law was put into effect in 1974 and applies to any school that received funds from the U.S. Department of Education. This law was designed to protect the privacy of a child's education records. Under this law, any score, grade, or GPA of a student, needs to be kept confidential. Only you and that student have the right to access these records, whether they are digital or physical. This means grades cannot be posted for others to see, even brothers. So for scenario #1 - NO, you cannot legally give Joey's grade to his brother. But what about a parent? Parents DO have the right to access student data IF the student is under the age of 18. Once the student turns 18 or attends a postsecondary education institution, they are sole owners of their data and it cannot be accessed by parents or anyone else.

FERPA goes into detail about what constitutes private data and how it can be shared and to whom. It is my recommendation that you read the act in its entirety rather than me providing you with legal information. Please go here to read the document:

https://www2.ed.gov/policy/gen/guid/fpco/ferpa/index.html

COPPA

COPPA stands for Children's Online Privacy Protection Act. This law is designed to protect the privacy of students under the age of 13, from online companies that collect data as part of their business. Many web providers collect information to either sell to 3rd party companies or to direct advertisements based on their demographics and interests. A site must acquire permission from the parent to legally collect personal data from a child under 13. So when considering scenario #2, the answer is - maybe, but maybe not. Before using any apps or websites, it is the teacher's responsibility to check the **Privacy Policy** of that provider. You can usually find this at the bottom of the page in small print or in the description page of the app. If the site says it collects private information and the permission of parents is required, then it is your responsibility to get that permission in writing before using the site or app. If it says it does not collect private data then you are safe to use the product. But what if your students are in 8th grade and over the age of 13? In this case, the provider must disclose that they do in fact collect personal data, but once someone reaches the age of 13, they can give their own consent. Some districts have strict policies in place regarding the use of any site or app that collects personal data, so be sure to check with yours before using such sites.

So what about using social media in your classroom? When I teach the laws of social media to my elementary students I inevitably get a very quiet room with big-eyed students. According to COPPA, no student should have a social media account if they are under the age of 13. Each platform states in its Privacy Policy that its website, products, and services are all directed to people who are at least 13 years or older. The only way these students could have made social media accounts is if they lied about their age upon registration. (Big eyes happen here when they know I caught them). This is when I explain to them how companies can access their information, what they do with that information, and if children are caught in violation of these laws, they can be banned from the platform. So I stress the importance of waiting until they are 13. It's also important to be honest about their age because platforms are required by law to keep children's identities private under the age of 18. Most sites will not allow a child's account to be searched and found by the general public if under 18.

What happens if a teacher is caught in violation of these federal laws? They (their school or district) can lose federal funding, and they can find themselves in civil litigation. More likely than not, the teacher would lose their job and possibly their license to teach. These laws are not to be taken lightly and every teacher needs to thoroughly understand them!

COPPA is a large influencer on the technology tools utilized in a classroom so you should read and be familiar with this law. Go to https://www.ecfr.gov/current/title-16/chapter-I/subchapter-C/part-312 to read the rule in its entirety.

CIPA

CIPA stands for Children's Internet Protection Act. We all understand the enormous cost of keeping the latest and fastest technology in classrooms and libraries so our children can continue learning the skills necessary to be successful in a technical world. This is why the US government created a universal services fund that schools and libraries can apply for to receive federal funding and maintain this ever-growing expanse of technology. This fund is called E-Rate. CIPA imposes technology protection measures on schools and libraries that receive E-Rate funding.

These institutions must educate children on appropriate online behavior, monitor the online activity of minors, and block or filter

Internet access to content that would otherwise be accessible to minors that is:

1. Obscene
2. Contains pornography
3. Could be harmful to minors

So let's consider scenario #3 again. Although it is sometimes unfortunate that "good" content is blocked due to trigger words or advertisements, this is a necessary procedure that schools and libraries must do to qualify for E-Rate funding. These filters are always getting better and with a domain administrator that is constantly modifying the parameters of these filters, hopefully, the good and the bad can be filtered appropriately. But in the meantime, yes, these filters are appropriate for the school to have in place.

Again, I am not providing legal advice so I am highly recommending all teachers and administrators to be familiar with these 3 laws to keep their students safe and to maintain the highest integrity for their institution. Please read the CIPA law here:

https://www.fcc.gov/consumers/guides/childrens-internet-protection-act

Reflect for your Eportfolio

1. If you have not already done so, go here to read about FERPA: https://www2.ed.gov/policy/gen/guid/fpco/ferpa/index.html

2. Whether you are a current teacher or future teacher, consider how you should keep student records.

    a. Is your grade book locked up when you leave your desk or is it sitting open for anyone to see?

    b. If you use a digital grade book, is this site/page open on your computer at all times or do you log out when you are not accessing it?

    c. Do you post student grades for others to see?

    d. Do you communicate with other teachers about student data over email?

3. Go to https://www.ecfr.gov/current/title-16/chapter-I/subchapter-C/part-312 to read about COPPA.

    a. Go to any game or education website. Scroll to the very bottom of the page and find their Privacy Policy.

    b. If your students are under the age of 13, can they use this platform?

    c. Would you need to get parental consent first?

I think you will be surprised how many education sites are NOT intended for use by students under the age of 13.

4. Go to
   https://www.fcc.gov/consumers/guides/childrens-internet-protecti
   on-act to read about CIPA.

   a. What are your thoughts on schools and libraries blocking
      YouTube?

5. Create a Google Doc to write about each of these 3 laws and how
   they affect your (future) classroom.

15 A Win-Win for Teachers and Students - *Teach and Learn with Digital Assessments*

Sarah teaches 8th-grade science. She has posters of the bones of the human body placed around her room. She has presented videos that demonstrate how joints work, she has students read from their textbooks and look at diagrams about each bone, and she has had many lectures while demonstrating with her life-size skeleton model that cheerfully wears a Santa hat all year long. She feels she had covered the content in detail but the results from her students' last quiz were fair at best.

think

Where did she go wrong? Are her students not paying attention? Did she miss something? What are her students not understanding?

This happens to all teachers. We think we covered the material thoroughly but our students are just not getting it!

I have high hopes for the advancements in technology, but in this day and age, we cannot see into the minds of our students enough to understand what they learn and what they don't learn. The only way for us to see what is going on inside our students' minds is for them to demonstrate their understanding. This means they must be assessed.

There are three ways of assessing student learning:

Diagnostic assessment is finding out what the students already know about a topic. By assessing their prior knowledge, the teacher has a better idea of what to teach his/her students and has a base score to compare to later.

Formative assessment is evaluating student progress as they continue to work. Teachers can provide feedback that will potentially help students' level of success and learning. Formative assessment should happen multiple times throughout the lesson.

Summative assessment is evaluating student progress at the end of instruction compared with the beginning of instruction. This is a gauge of total knowledge on the subject.

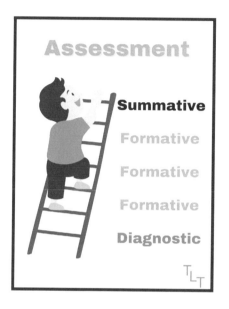

Image available at https://www.teachandlearnwithtechnology.com/resources

Teachers of large classes or many students find it difficult to provide assessments, grade the assessments and get feedback to the students in a timely manner so the instruction can be modified according to the results. In traditional paper and pencil classrooms, this can take up to two days minimum. One day to take the assessment and one day to disperse the results and continue forward based on these results. This often means the teacher is grading in the evenings on their personal time and when the students return the following day, the students often forget how they answered the questions in the first place. Oftentimes students only look at the number right and wrong instead of WHAT they got right or wrong. This is so important when it comes to students learning from their mistakes.

By using technology to assess students, the assessment can be dispersed and submitted digitally to avoid the physical aspect of the paper. But even better than this, the assessment is immediately compared to the answer key and is graded upon hitting the submit button. This takes the hours of grading out of the equation and eliminates the time between performance and feedback.

For example, John is one of Sarah's students. On a paper assessment, he didn't know if the correct bone was the radius or the ulna. He took a random guess and it was correct. When he receives his score back the following day, he sees he got 8 of 10 correct but doesn't put together which ones were wrong and which were right. He's just happy with the 8 out of 10.

If John takes the same assessment digitally, he will know immediately that his guess was correct and he will know the correct answer in the future.

Some tech tools look and act much like a paper assessment. They may have multiple choice, fill in the blank or essay questions. The assessment may be graded after each question or graded at the end of the completed assessment. These will depend on the platform and the options available to the teacher upon creation. These are commonly used as summative assessments.

Other assessment tech tools might not even look like an assessment and you may not have to tell your students it's an assessment at all, because it appears to be a game. We talked about the advantages that gamification has in the classroom in Chapter 8 and how much students enjoy playing games. Games can be a great form of diagnostic or formative assessment.

What makes these even nicer is the student is intrinsically motivated to perform well so they can advance within the game setting, where oftentimes an assessment that looks and acts like a traditional test is based on extrinsic motivation. And let's be honest - games are just FUN!

 Tech Tools

Sarah found some ways to utilize technology for all three types of assessments. When her class enters the room, she has a QR code on her projector. Her students scan the code and take a short, two-question quiz in Google Forms asking which image is the ulna and which is the radius. This diagnostic quiz is immediately graded and she can see the results popping up on her screen within seconds of the student completing it. She sees only about half of her class gets it correct, so she addressed the difference between these two bones and the ways they can remember each at the very beginning of class. Her students then play an interactive game online that lets students practice placing the bones on the human body.

- There are many of these available online. Here are just a couple: http://www.tenalpscommunicate.com/clients/siemens/humanbodyOnline/#
- https://www.abcya.com/games/skeletal_system
- https://www.dairy.edu.au/build-a-skeleton

Each student gets immediate feedback on their answer so they can correct it and learn from their mistake.

While her classroom continues to work, Sarah is addressing other classroom happenings like a student coming in late, another student that can't find their notebook, and a teacher from across the hall wanting to borrow her highlighter. (Let's be real - this is our day!)

If students got stuck, they could refer to the textbook, videos, or posters around the room. So students can continue to learn, and have fun and students are intrinsically motivated to improve their scores.

At the end of class, she asks how many students scored less than two minutes on the game. The majority of her class raised their hands telling her they were getting the answers correct. She then showed the same QR code and gave the same ulna and radius quiz from the beginning of class. 99% of her students got it correct. She can see on her screen which of her students missed it so she was able to address him/her before the bell rang.

The next day she did the same thing with the tibia and fibula but had her students play a different game. On Friday, all of her students played a game of Kahoot.com that included all the bones they had learned about that week. She could see from the reports of the game which students were struggling and what content students were struggling with the most. She could see her 2nd hour really struggled with the questions about joints but her 4th hour didn't understand the bones of the hand. She could adjust how she taught each class based on these reports.

In this scenario, Sarah and her students could receive immediate feedback and the game adjusts based on their performance. This is how teachers can meet their students where they are and differentiate for students' needs. Of course, her students will have fun learning the standards within a short amount of time and students like John, will immediately know if his guess was correct or not. A win-win!

So what if her students all passed the ulna/radius quiz at the beginning of the class? Great! Now she knows they got that and she could move on to the quiz about the tibia and fibula.

Digital assessments given at the right times can provide both the teacher and student with immediate feedback based on their results.

☞ Reflect for your Eportfolio

There are many free digital assessment tools online. CommonSense.org has The Top Tech Tools for Formative Assessment.

This page is maintained and kept up with the latest tools online. I appreciate the grade band recommendation for each tool and the star reviews based on set criteria.

1. Explore this page and find a new tech tool to implement in your classroom.

2. Based on the new tool you find on this page, do you think these digital assessments would be a clear reflection of student knowledge?

3. Create a Google Doc with an explanation of the tool you selected, what type of assessment it is best suited for, and if you could get a clear assessment of student understanding. You may want to include screenshots of your tool.

16 Not IF But WHEN - *Basic Troubleshooting and Maintenance of Classroom Technology*

Troubleshooting

If you have technology, it will inevitably need some upkeep. Although technology can look intimidating at first, there are some simple things you can do to keep things running smoothly. Schools will often have mismatched technology due to the year things were purchased. This can be because technology is always changing and updating but also because the funding available is different at separate purchase dates. The very same technology can often come with their individual ailments to them. One may not connect to the Internet while another crashes suddenly just before saving a project. While these are often time-consuming to rejuvenate, it is often well worth the effort.

If your technology isn't working correctly, your first step is to approach your building technology team to see what the process is for tech support. Some schools and districts have designated personnel trained to repair and maintain the technology in a particular building whereas others don't have the resources for that and the teachers are expected to do their own. If you are fortunate enough to have IT people in your building, put in your repair request and be patient. Speaking from experience, these people have a LOT of things on their plate, so although it may not get done "yesterday", your politeness and appreciation will go a long way when it comes to getting it done! If you have a building-level IT department, don't try to fix it yourself. This will often make the process drag out even further if they have to undo something you have done.

If you don't have building-level IT, ask an administrator if it's appropriate to contact the district IT department or if your office staff is the contact. Schools generally have a long chain of command and if you overstep the wrong people, it may put you further down the list, and no one wants that.

If you find out teachers are responsible for repairing their own technology, there are some simple things to start with.

- My favorite fix in the whole world is the turn-it-off and back-on trick. It seems so silly but somehow when things reboot, they often fix themselves. **Always try this first!**

- Sometimes the easiest way to find a fix is to compare it to a device that is working properly. As you go through the list below, compare these to a device that is working. *Make sure not to make any changes to the working device!*

- If it's an app or piece of software that isn't working correctly, close it out completely and try opening it again. On a MAC computer this means not only clicking the red dot on the top but going to File>Quit or Command+Q. On an iPad, you will need to swipe the app out to completely close it. Due to operating system (OS) updates, this process looks a little different each time a new update comes out, but if you Google how to close out an app for your OS you should find directions on how to do it.

- If a program was working yesterday and doesn't work today, it may be because the OS automatically updated, or maybe it needs an update. Check that the OS is the same on both a working and non-working device.

- Check the software or app version are the same. One may be newer and one may be older and need an update.

- Check all cords. A cord that isn't in the correct port or got unplugged can be a simple fix for your Internet, printer, or projector not connecting.

- If all settings and cords appear to be the same on working and non-working devices, you may want to switch out a cord and see if that changes anything. Sometimes a cord or adapter (often called a dongle) goes bad and needs to be replaced.

- If things still aren't working correctly, try talking to other teachers with similar devices. They can either tell you how to correct the situation or where to go for help. Never underestimate the knowledge of your office staff! They may be able to point you in the right direction too.

- **DON'T make any changes in the Settings, System Preferences, or Control Panel!** This is just a place to look at and compare the working with the non-working. Changes here are better left to trained personnel.

- **DON'T attempt to open any device up or get into the electronics parts.** This not only runs the risk of electrical shock but also voids most manufacturer warranties.

These are basic troubleshooting techniques you can also teach your students. Teachers that assign student jobs will often put those tech-savvy students in charge of classroom IT. Again, they should not be changing settings anywhere, but they can absolutely do the things listed above.

Maintenance

Technology needs basic upkeep to run smoothly. Everyday maintenance will include things like charging and cleaning.

If a device is rarely used, charge it fully and then shut it down. It may or may not hold the charge while it sits idle, but don't leave it on until it drains the battery.

If the device is used frequently, then be sure to recharge it every night while the students are gone. Some batteries lose their ability to hold a charge if they are plugged in continuously. This is particularly common with robotics. Be sure to read the instructions for each device. In these cases, I usually plug them in when I leave at the end of the day and leave myself a note to unplug them when I get back in the next morning. I won't leave these batteries plugged in over a weekend or for multiple days. Eventually, they won't hold a charge at all. Computers and tablets can usually be left plugged in for extended times. Over long holidays, spring break, or summer I make sure all devices are completely powered down.

If you have ever taken a close look at a seven-year-old's hands (I'm not necessarily suggesting this), you will know they carry remnants of the playground, the tacos served at lunch, the paint used in art class, and whatever products the human body produces! I have had students using hand sanitizer (I call it "germ juice") when they walk into my classroom for fifteen years now. When COVID took the world by storm, the use of hand sanitizer in schools went through the roof. Many students couldn't tolerate the constant exposure to the harsh chemicals on their skin all day and developed rashes or excessively dry skin. I asked these students to wash their hands before using technology while the rest of the students continued to use germ juice before picking up their devices. Even though this was a routine, it didn't keep the black film from slowly developing on the keyboards or the sneezes that ended up on screens.

Side note - Teach all students how to sneeze in their sleeves at the beginning of the year.

Cleaning technology is not something I usually let students do for a number of reasons.

If even the smallest amount of moisture gets into a device, it can stop working. For example, tablets and/or cases on tablets are infamous for getting dirty from frequent use. Company websites discourage the use of wet wipes for cleaning and suggest a dry cloth. My guess is these companies have never seen a first graders tablet in May! I would use a wet wipe but before using it, squeeze as much excess liquid out of the wipe as possible. Then I would shut the device completely down and unplug it if necessary. I would begin by wiping the sealed parts of the device like the casing. Once the wipe had dried out a little, then I would gently and carefully wipe around the parts that had openings, such as the ports, buttons, speakers, and camera, making sure no liquid got inside. I did this with computer keyboards and mouse as well.

Side note - The plural form for computer mouse is not mice. Mouse stands for Manually-Operated User-Selection Equipment, which means it is already plural. It is equipment, so it is "mouse". ●

Make sure everything is completely dry before plugging it back in and turning it on. If in doubt, clean it at the end of the day and wait until the next day to power it back up.

One of my technology expectations (from Chapter 6) is to keep all food and liquid away from technology. Unfortunately, it is usually the teachers that have the hardest time with this because they are often multitasking during lunchtime or having that morning cup of coffee. **If liquid gets spilled on a keyboard or device, unplug it immediately!** If you can shut it down, do this as soon as possible. **Do not continue to use it wet!** If it's a keyboard, turn it upside down so the liquid can drain back out the keys rather than allowing the liquid to sit on the electronics. If it's sticky soda or juice, unfortunately, this is usually a death sentence for technology. It usually can't be cleaned internally enough to work properly again. If it's water or black coffee, sometimes it will work again after completely drying out but even then, you may not have all keys functioning properly.

If a tablet gets dropped into water or is spilled on, shut it down immediately, set the device so any openings (charging port, camera, etc) are facing down, and place it in a sealed bag of dry rice for a week or so. These devices are often fairly resilient and may recover from getting wet.

If a device gets dropped or breaks, the teacher should be the one to pick it up. **Students should not pick up a broken device. Be very careful when picking it up!** Broken devices can have sharp pieces of glass, metal, or plastic. Collect all pieces, document the incident, and report it to your IT department and your administrator. **Do not throw anything away!** Everything purchased through a school is done so through public funding. These items are likely to be on an inventory that tracks these funds and must go through a documented process before discarding them. Some districts repurpose broken devices or part them out to fix other devices.

Installing and Deleting Software

Due to security and privacy, most schools and districts are very careful about what software, apps, and even websites students and staff use while on campus. One bad software installation could bring down the server for the entire district, not to mention allow access to personal information to those that shouldn't have it. Although it is often a tedious process, installs should be approved by the building or district tech department to avoid such catastrophes. If this is not in place where you are, chances are good that a device not working properly or just doing odd things has malware or a virus messing things up. Again, this is not something you should try to tackle on your own. Most districts have a procedure they must follow to diagnose and remove these problems so your job is to communicate to someone what is happening.

If you are having trouble with a specific app or program, try checking with other teachers also using it in their classrooms. Depending on the program, this may or may not be something your building IT department can assist you with. Sometimes they are trained on a specific piece of software if it's for testing or mandated as part of a curriculum, but if you found a website and want to use it in your classroom, your IT department may not be the expert for it. In this case, you may need to contact the company's support team either by phone, email, or through their support page. You may want to communicate your issue with your IT department so they are in the know, but anything you can resolve yourself is one less thing for them!

The best way to avoid having to troubleshoot or do deep maintenance is to follow and enforce your classroom expectations about technology use. If students and staff are not allowed to change settings, remove cords, install or remove apps and software, etc, it narrows down the possibilities when something goes wrong.

Remember, not if, but when technology goes array, keep the mindset that it can be fixed, have a positive attitude, and portray patience to your students and staff about it getting resolved. This will not only teach your students how to have a growth mindset but you will feel better when you leave at the end of the day.

17 "YES! This is the Kind of Teacher I Want Working at My School!" - Creating a Professional Digital Portfolio

Eportfolio

Travis is a newly graduated college student with an education degree in secondary English Language Arts. He has found a number of job openings for the next school year so he applies to their online application. He knows he is in a high competition area with many applicants that apply for teaching jobs where he lives.

think

How can Travis stand out from the other applicants as a first-year teacher?

Application demonstrates true knowledge and understanding.

Some teaching jobs are highly competitive. Oftentimes getting into some of the top school districts is slim unless you have teaching experience. Just like any job, your application needs to stand out amongst the others to get an interview. Outside of providing the traditional resume and application, one of the best ways to demonstrate your knowledge of the teaching field and display your experience is to create a portfolio. In college, students produce a plethora of lessons, and activities, take images of classroom experiences, and can even have a collection of student work. Organizing these artifacts into a digital format provides a nice way to showcase your knowledge and experience when applying for teaching positions.

A digital portfolio or **eportfolio** (electronic portfolio) is an online collection of your work that shows evidence of your knowledge and understanding of the teaching field. Due to its digital nature, it can demonstrate your ability to integrate technology into education. It is also a reflection of your personality, creativity, and interests. By sharing a link to your eportfolio, you are providing a small window into what you are capable of doing. If you have read this book in its entirety or taken technology integration courses, you have knowledge other applicants don't. If you have taken classes to learn the fundamentals of classroom management, teaching theory, and application and specifically understand the pedagogy behind technology integration, creating an eportfolio puts you a step ahead of other applicants.

Your eportfolio needs to be in an organized and accessible location. I have found the best place for an eportfolio is to create a website.

Throughout this book, there are sections dedicated to "Reflect for your Eportfolio". If you have been doing these, then this is a great start for your eportfolio but you are not limited to only this..

 Tech Tools

 Google Sites

Google Sites is yet another free app within the Google Apps Suite that allows anyone to drag and drop content into a user-friendly interface. You can have a fully customizable, published website up in a short amount of time. As you begin formatting your site and adding content, I suggest you are always asking yourself **"What kind of person do I want administrators to see?"** You have the ability to use images, videos, formatting, projects, lesson plans, and things you have specifically learned in a classroom that cannot be shared adequately on an application. An administrator wants to know if you are the kind of person they want working in their school. Be thoughtful of colors, themes, and the mood you portray. You should not be sharing personal information such as your home life. It should be professional. It should be free of grammar and spelling errors. This reflects poorly on teachers in general. Be sure to use your tools to check for accuracy.

Your eportfolio should be EASY to understand and navigate. Rather than including text links to items, try **embedding** them into your site. This means the artifact will be displayed within a window directly on your site, rather than the viewer leaving your page to see it. If an administrator or review committee is quickly scrolling through your page, they are less likely to click on a link and more likely to see an image. Consider the two options below:

Text link appearance	Embedded object appearance
Technology Use Poster	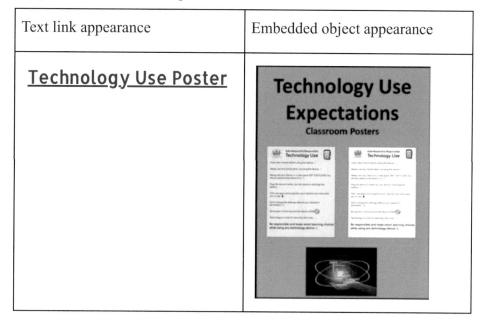

We will then discuss how to navigate your site after your items have been added. You will create your eportfolio with a theme but don't worry about formatting (colors and fonts) until you have your content added. I tell my students not to "decorate their cake before baking it." This means they need the ingredients put together before they can start making it look good.

 Create Your Eportfolio

1. Make sure you are logged into your Google account and go to https://sites.google.com/
2. Create a new site using your name or your name + eportfolio as the title. Continue to add content from each of the previous chapters.

 Watch this video about how to start your site

Recommendations for eportfolio content:

1. Cover/welcome page and Index with links to all topics
2. All about me page including:

    a. Professional-looking photo of you

    b. Write about your teaching interests and why

    c. Contact info including email and social media

3. Your philosophy of technology in the classroom as it relates to technology integration

4. EMBED your vision board (Chapter 1)

    a. Your thoughts on a growth mindset for both you and your students

    b. Your thoughts about having goals (What are your professional goals?)

5. How Google Apps can benefit your classroom (Chapter 2)

6. Evaluation of a tech tool using current theories (Chapter 3)

    a. The Triple E Framework (X2)

    b. The 4 C's (+3 Cs)

    c. SAMR Model

7. The importance of a PLN and evidence of your participation (Chapter 4)

8. ISTE standards (Chapter 5)

    a. Your ISTE Standards for Educators mind map and how you are meeting these standards (or working on meetings) these standards

    b. The ISTE Standards for Students and who should teach them

9. Your established classroom routine for 1:1 technology (Chapter 6)

10. Compare with Low-Tech/No-Tech (Chapter 7)

11. Discuss gamification and include your screenshot (Chapter 8)

12. Discuss audio and video in your classroom. Include your audio file link and QR code and clean-viewing video site (Chapter 9)

13. EMBED your Chatterpix video (Chapter 10)

    a. You may also want to include AR, VR, and virtual field trips

14. STEM, computational thinking, and coding with your screenshot (Chapter 11)

15. Assistive Technology (Chapter 12)

16. Digital citizenship in your future classroom (Chapter 13)

17. Review the 3 federal laws for student privacy (Chapter 14)

18. Digital assessment (Chapter 15)

19. Include other evidence of your teaching and/or technology integration knowledge:

    a. EMBED a lesson plan you developed

    b. Include a digital assessment specific to this lesson

    c. Scan copies of student work

    d. Photos* (see note below)

    e. Screenshot mentor teacher comments

    f. etc…

Include anything an administrator would see value in and show them your capabilities as an educator at their school.

*If you use any images from the web be sure to cite them with a URL

*If you have practicum lessons or photos, these are great to include but be very careful not to include student's faces.

A Google Doc check sheet is available to download at
https://www.teachandlearnwithtechnology.com/resources

 <u>Watch this video about how to publish your site</u>

An eportfolio is a digital collection of your work and allows you to brag about your abilities as a teacher. It can make you stand out above other candidates so that when an administrator reviews your application, they can say "Yes! This is the kind of teacher I want working at my school!"

Now that you have your content, it is important an administrator or hiring team can easily navigate your site without missing content or getting lost. You should include an index on the front page of your eportfolio. This is a collection of quick links to your other pages, similar to a table of contents.

When considering the navigation of your site, it may be helpful to draw a mind map (or use the website I shared in chapter 1) to map out your site. When moving around on a site it is easiest if similar content is grouped together on the same page. Then provide a link to that page explaining what will be found there, in your index rather than depending on the menu. The video below will explain why.

 Watch this video about how to add an index to your site

Your eportfolio is a dynamic and creative representation of you and your ability to integrate technology into your classroom. I hope it helps land you your first or your next teaching position. Until then, continue to maintain this eportfolio and keep it up to date as you progress through college, acquire experience, and expand your ability to Teach and Learn with Technology.

Epilogue

As you complete this book, I invite you to reflect on your journey.

- What was your mindset about integrating technology into your classroom before you started this process? Were you fearful or at the least hesitant?
- Had you experienced or heard of things going wrong with technology with students and wanting to avoid such incidents at all costs?
- Did you know how to judge whether your resources were beneficial to your students?
- Were you prepared to teach your students how to be safe while online?
- Did you have a collection of content ready to present to prospective administrators?

Your road to a successful classroom is like no others. Yet we are all on the same education bus for one purpose: **To prepare students with the necessary skills to be successful now, next year, after graduation, and in whatever they pursue in life.**

With each passing day, we see the rise in technology advances. From the medical field to the military to the self-check-out systems at the grocery store. Technology is ever-changing AND IT SHOULD BE! Our future needs people to develop, maintain and improve upon our expanding technological world. This is the jobs of tomorrow. YOU are teaching the future leaders of tomorrow!

This book is not the end of your journey toward technology integration in your classroom, but rather the end of the beginning. My hope is that this book encourages you to step out of your comfort zone, explore other technology resources and take advantage of opportunities you would have otherwise passed by.

I do not wish you luck. Oprah Winfrey said "I believe luck is preparation meeting opportunity. If you hadn't been prepared when the opportunity came along, you wouldn't have been lucky."

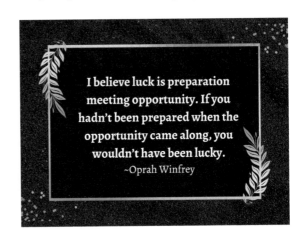

I do wish you all fast Internet speeds, search results on page one, and of course an ever-growing mindset.

~Jill

References

ABCya (n.d) https://www.abcya.com/games/skeletal_system

Anderson, B. M. (2020, January 9). *The most in-demand hard and soft skills of 2020*. LinkedIn. https://www.linkedin.com/business/talent/blog/talent-strategy/linkedin-most-in-demand-hard-and-soft-skills

Bloom, B., & et. al. (2001). *Blooms taxonomy :: Resource for educators*. Blooms Taxonomy :: Resource for Educators. From https://bloomstaxonomy.net/

CIPA (2019, December) Children's Internet Protection Act (CIPA) https://www.fcc.gov/consumers/guides/childrens-internet-protection-act

Classdojo.com. (n.d) *Growth Mindset - Big Ideas - Classdojo*. Classdojo. https://ideas.classdojo.com/b/growth-mindset/
Code.org (n.d) https://www.dictionary.com/browse/technology

Common Sense Media. (n.d.). *You know your kids.we know media and tech.* https://www.commonsensemedia.org/about-us/our-mission

COPPA (2013, January) PART 312 - CHILDREN'S ONLINE PRIVACY PROTECTION RULE https://www.ecfr.gov/current/title-16/chapter-I/subchapter-C/part-312

Dairy.edu.au (n.d.). https://www.dairy.edu.au/build-a-skeleton

Darling-Hammond, L., & et al. (2013, June). *Criteria for high quality assessment*. The Association of Test Publishers. https://www.testpublishers.org/

Dweck, C. S. (2008). *Mindset: The New Psychology Of Success.* Ballantine Books.

FERPA (1997, March). https://nces.ed.gov/pubs97/web/97859.asp
FERPA (2021, August). https://www2.ed.gov/policy/gen/guid/fpco/ferpa/index.html

Global Reach. (2020, January 28). *The 2nd largest search engine on the internet*. Global Reach. https://www.globalreach.com/global-reach-media/blog/2020/01/28/the-2nd-largest-search-engine-on-the-internet

Heffernan, V. (2017, November 15). *Just google it: A short history of a newfound verb*. Wired., https://www.wired.com/story/just-google-it-a-short-history-of-a-newfound-verb/

IDEA (n.d.). https://sites.ed.gov/idea/about-idea/

ISTE (2022). *ISTE Computational Thinking Competencies*. https://www.iste.org/standards/iste-standards-for-computational-thinking

Kahn Academy. (2014, August 19). *Growing your mind*. YouTube. https://www.youtube.com/watch?v=WtKJrB5rOKs&feature=youtu.be

Kahoot (n.d.). https://kahoot.com/

Kolb, L. (2020, December 9). *Triple E framework*. Triple E Framework. https://www.tripleeframework.com/

Merriam-Webster. (n.d.). Technology. In *Merriam-Webster.com dictionary*.
https://www.merriam-webster.com/dictionary/technology

Puentedura, R. R. (2010). *SAMR and TPCK: Intro to advanced practice - hippasus*. SAMR and TPCK: Intro to Advanced Practice.
http://hippasus.com/resources/sweden2010/SAMR_TPCK_IntroToAdvancedPractice.pdf

Sieman (n.d.).
http://www.tenalpscommunicate.com/clients/siemens/humanbodyOnline/#

Scratch (n.d.). *https://scratch.mit.edu/*

Tucker, A. and Belford, . Geneva G. (2022, August 24). *computer science. Encyclopedia Britannica*.
https://www.britannica.com/science/computer-science

Images

https://pixabay.com/vectors/classroom-presentation-school-1297780/

https://upload.wikimedia.org/wikipedia/commons/e/e7/Right-pointing_hand_in_green_octagon.svg

https://pixabay.com/vectors/play-button-audio-symbol-player-30619/

https://upload.wikimedia.org/wikipedia/commons/b/bf/Blue_question_mark_%28italic%29.svg

https://pixabay.com/vectors/check-check-mark-red-mark-tick-303494/

https://upload.wikimedia.org/wikipedia/commons/e/e0/Tools_clipart.png

http://www.freestockphotos.biz/stockphoto/14223

https://docs.google.com/document/d/1YcgnLzgt_bhXQdyAPavObcq_QTXRna
qsg_MQvvl_7CM/edit#

https://docs.google.com/document/d/1YcgnLzgt_bhXQdyAPavObcq_QTXRna
qsg_MQvvl_7CM/edit#

https://docs.google.com/document/d/1YcgnLzgt_bhXQdyAPavObcq_QTXRna
qsg_MQvvl_7CM/edit#

https://docs.google.com/document/d/1YcgnLzgt_bhXQdyAPavObcq_QTXRna
qsg_MQvvl_7CM/edit#

https://docs.google.com/document/d/1YcgnLzgt_bhXQdyAPavObcq_QTXRna
qsg_MQvvl_7CM/edit#

https://commons.wikimedia.org/wiki/File:Think_Company_Logo,_small.png

https://pixabay.com/illustrations/bulb-idea-bright-lamp-light-3118633/

https://twitter.com/

https://www.instagram.com/

https://docs.google.com/document/d/1YcgnLzgt_bhXQdyAPavObcq_QTXRna
qsg_MQvvl_7CM/edit#

https://docs.google.com/document/d/1YcgnLzgt_bhXQdyAPavObcq_QTXRna
qsg_MQvvl_7CM/edit#

https://pixabay.com/photos/action-adult-paralympics-prosthetic-1867014/

https://docs.google.com/document/d/1YcgnLzgt_bhXQdyAPavObcq_QTXRna
qsg_MQvvl_7CM/edit#heading=h.43ah2wtwey0x

https://pixabay.com/photos/ipad-technology-tablet-1126136/

https://www.flickr.com/photos/dogtrax/44125197650

https://www.pexels.com/photo/young-lady-learning-sign-language-during-online-lesson-with-female-tutor-7516363/

https://www.pexels.com/photo/a-woman-and-a-young-girl-using-a-tablet-7943950/

https://pixabay.com/vectors/mental-health-cranium-head-human-3350778/

About The Author

Jill Outka-Hill is a certified educator of 24 years. She has taught preschool through adult technology, STEM, and software training classes.

She holds a teaching degree from the University of Wyoming, a master's in Technology in Education from Lesley University, a graduate endorsement from Black Hills State University in English as a New Language, and a graduate endorsement in K12 Instructional Technology from Arizona Technology in Education Association.

Jill is an ISTE Certified Educator, Google Certified Trainer, and Apple Certified Teacher.

www.teachandlearnwithtechnology.com

https://twitter.com/jilloutkahill

Notes

Notes

Notes

Notes

Notes

Made in the USA
Thornton, CO
01/09/24 14:11:24